# His treasured possession

## What kind of people ought we to be?

Lynette G. Clark

DayOne

©Day One Publications 2019

First printed 2019

ISBN 978-1-84625-639-4

All Scripture quotations, unless stated otherwise, are from the NIV 2011.

A CIP record is held at the British Library

Published by Day One Publications, Ryelands Road, Leominster, HR6 8NZ

☎ 01568 613 740

FAX 01568 611 473

email—sales@dayone.co.uk

web site—www.dayone.co.uk

Cover design by Kathryn Chedgzoy

Printed by 4edge Limited

To my beloved husband, Stephen,
whom I have had the privilege
to love and walk with for over forty years,
and who has been to me throughout that time
'as iron sharpening iron' (Proverbs 27:17);

And to my dearest sister, Susie,
whom I followed in the faith within
weeks of her conversion,
and whose love has meant so much to me.

'Godliness' and 'holiness' are words that seem to have fallen out of the Christian vocabulary these days. Lynette Clark has to be congratulated in bringing these concepts to the attention of the twenty-first-century Christian. Her work is biblical, practical and, above all, accessible. Anecdotes, quotations and verbal illustrations help to bring her theology to life and ensure that it is down-to-earth and real. Each chapter concludes with searching and practical questions which make the book useful for serious study, as well as for book groups or home-group programmes. The appendices are encyclopaedic and enrich the content. This book is a must for today's Christians and today's churches. Soli Deo gloria.

**Sheila Stephen, Visiting Lecturer at Union School of Theology, Bryntirion**

*This book is an accessible, engaging, biblical walk through different aspects of the Christian life, from our own interior spirituality through to its outward expression in hospitality and evangelism. The chapters are peppered with helpful illustrations, including some that are very personal and moving. Lynette manages to be searching and challenging without being heavy or hectoring, and the whole is permeated by a warm spirit of gratitude to God for his finished work. The chapters would repay slow reading, perhaps one a day, not because they are complicated, but because they are so practical (there are even recipes to help the culinarily incompetent make a start with hospitality!). For the new Christian they will be like the first visit to the gym that Lynette recounts; for the frequent visitor they will be like a friend's reminder to revisit regularly the fundamentals of Christian discipleship.*

**Revd Dr Garry Williams, Director of, and lecturer at, the Pastors' Academy; visiting Professor of Historical Theology at Westminster Theological Seminary (Philadelphia); Adjunct Professor of Historical Theology at Puritan Reformed Theological Seminary (Michigan); and an ordained elder at Christchurch, Harpenden**

### Godliness:
### *value for all things*

*. . . train yourself to be godly. For physical training is of some value, but* godliness *has value for* all *things, holding promise for both the present life and the life to come.*
(*1 Timothy 4:7b–8*)

*For you are a people holy to the* LORD *your God. The* LORD *your God has chosen you out of all the peoples on the face of the earth to be his people, his treasured possession.*
(*Deuteronomy 7:6*)

# Contents

# Acknowledgements

I am indebted to Anne Rees of Swansea, who was the first of a number of women who encouraged me to transcribe my notes on 'godliness' into a book. Without that initial suggestion this book might never have been written.

I am very much in the debt of Donald Mitchell, Librarian at Union School of Theology. He saved me from weeks of work by tracking down the sources of many of the quotations in this book. A thousand thanks. Thanks also go to the memory of Rhian Middleton of the Evangelical Movement of Wales office, who in 2018 went to be with her Lord, and who painstakingly ploughed through numerous copies of the EMW magazine to find 'just those things I needed': her deeds will follow her (Revelation 14:13).

My gratitude to Brenda Lewis, formerly of the Evangelical Movement of Wales, and to Anne Davies, of the Christian bookshop in Bala, knows no bounds: to Brenda, for her checking of the original manuscript; and to Anne, for her personal prayer support and encouragement. I acknowledge my indebtedness to Pastor Philip Williams, who suggested a number of constructive alterations to my manuscript.

I would especially like to express my thanks to Tim Mattox, pastor of Calvary Chapel in Paphos, Cyprus. I wrote this book while I was with my husband who was on sabbatical at the Neapolis University of Cyprus. For four months we were greatly privileged to sit, Sunday by Sunday, under Tim's preaching: it was scriptural, simple, searching, Saviour-focused, spiritual ministry. Again and again we felt that Tim had been eclipsed by our great Saviour Himself and that we were 'sitting at the feet of Jesus'. What a great blessing and help!

I would like to thank all the staff at the Neapolis University, Paphos, for making our stay so enjoyable. A special 'thank you' goes to the library staff for all their help.

I am indebted to Lindsay Brown for his generous Foreword. That he found time in his very busy schedule not only to contribute this but also to make numerous helpful suggestions increases my sense of gratitude and indebtedness to him.

I am especially thankful to Mark Roberts and for Day One's response in publishing my book, and for all those who have helped in the process. My particular thanks go to Suzanne Mitchell, my copy-editor, for all her hard work and the helpful recommendations and suggestions she made.

Finally, I am grateful to two family members for their help and encouragement throughout. My dear sister Susie gave me much sound advice and made various helpful comments. I am also deeply indebted to my husband, Stephen, for his faithful ministry over so many years which has directed my gaze again and again to our wonderful Saviour.

I am grateful to all the aforementioned for their help. Any inaccuracies or infelicities of style are entirely mine.

Give thanks to the LORD, for he is good;
  his love endures for ever.
Let the redeemed of the LORD tell their story . . .
(Psalm 107:1–2a)

# Foreword

This is a little gem of a book. Lynette Clark offers a judicious mix of biblical insight and reflection, well-chosen stories, and apt quotations from great Christian saints of the past which left me frequently challenged. I often had to turn aside to reflect and pray over some of the challenges. Helpful questions at the end of each chapter bring the message home even more forcibly.

One of the great saints whom Lynette Clark is fond of quoting, the great theologian and pastor Samuel Rutherford, once wrote, 'My heart is not my own—Christ has run away to heaven with it.' This book develops the implications for the heart that has been captured by Jesus Christ, the King of heaven. The great theme and focus of the book revolves around the importance of putting down deep roots in Christ, and Lynette helpfully details the indicators of growth and depth in the Christian life for disciples of Jesus: growing in understanding the grace of God, following the path of godliness and obedience, deepening our knowledge of God, and learning to know him experientially, with all the implications that has for stewardship, contentment and bearing witness before the watching world. She provides a rich and elaborate tapestry. As I read through the text, it reminded me of these words from the great Protestant Reformer Martin Luther: 'If you knew what you were saved from, you would die of fear; but if you knew what you were saved for, you would die of joy.'

This book helpfully spells out the two sides of the coin of

Christian discipleship: on the one side, the oft-neglected call to godliness and obedience (I am struck by Jesus' words 'If you love me, keep my commands', John 14:15); and on the other side, the joy and sense of wonder that come from going deeper in our knowledge and experience of God.

For that reason, this book is best read one chapter at a time, perhaps even as a daily devotional, with opportunity to reflect on the questions at the end of each chapter. It provides a meditative and reflective study which can only enrich and deepen the experience of all those who read as determined followers of Jesus Christ. I am pleased to recommend it heartily. May you be enriched and challenged, as I was!

Lindsay Brown
Former General Secretary of the International
Fellowship of Evangelical Students, and former
International Director of the Lausanne Movement

# Preface

If we are Christians, our greatest desire should be to glorify God and to enjoy Him. One of the ways in which we can honour and glorify Him is in the manner in which we live before a watching world.

This book began life as a series of addresses delivered at a number of different conferences for ministers' wives. This explains why much of the content of the book, including the illustrations, is slanted towards women, although I hope that any male readers will also find this book helpful. My purpose and aim in writing it is simply (!) to encourage the Christian reader in the pursuit of godly living. Godliness is not packaged or automatic: it will not be found by lounging in a comfortable chair. We all need to be determined and tenacious in our desire to promote godliness in our own lives and in the lives of others. The 'Food for thought' questions at the end of each chapter are designed to encourage further reflection on the subject and are suitable for personal or group use.

Let us consider how we may spur one another on
towards love and good deeds. (Hebrews 10:24)

# Part 1. Value for all things

# 1 Getting started

*The Word became flesh and made his dwelling among us. We have seen his glory, the glory of the one and only Son, who came from the Father, full of grace and truth. (John 1:14)*

*[Grace] does away with the distance between the sinner and God, which sin had created. It meets the sinner on the spot where he stands; grace approaches him just as he is. [Grace] does not wait till there is something to attract it, nor till a good reason is found in the sinner for its flowing to him . . . It was free sovereign grace when it first thought of the sinner; it was free grace when it found and laid hold of him, and it is free grace when it hands him up into glory. (Horatius Bonar)*

None of us begins as a godly person; we were *all* ungodly. How does anyone become godly? It's down to two words: grace and salvation. Godliness is only possible because 'at just the right time, when we were still powerless, Christ died for the ungodly', and 'while we were still sinners, Christ died for us' (Romans 5:6, 8). And what Christ purchased for sinners, the Holy Spirit applies to those whom He brings to salvation: 'His divine power has given us everything we need for a godly life' (2 Peter 1:3). This is what salvation is: something procured *for* us by Christ and then applied *to* us, and *in* us, through His Holy Spirit.

And the cause of this? God's grace: that is to say, His free and undeserved favour and kindness shown to those who only deserve His wrath.

For the grace of God has appeared that offers salvation to all people. It teaches us to say 'No' to ungodliness and worldly passions, and to live self-controlled, upright and godly lives in this present age, while we wait for the blessed hope— the appearing of the glory of our great God and Saviour, Jesus Christ, who gave himself for us to redeem us from all wickedness and to purify for himself a people that are his very own, eager to do what is good. (Titus 2:11–14)

For us, therefore, this is a salvation which is 'from here to eternity'. But from God's perspective, it is something planned in eternity that reaches down in time and sweeps us up into His eternal and gracious purpose. Our new life in this age is *preparation* for our life in the age to come; in fact, the gift of salvation to us means that the new age has already begun to dawn in our lives: we await its consummation at the coming of the Lord. As a former generation of saints expressed it, 'Grace is glory begun below.'

Now I commit you to God and to the word of his grace, which can build you up and give you an inheritance among all those who are sanctified. (Acts 20:32)

## Food for thought

1. *How does anyone become godly?*
2. *To what are we to say 'No'?*
3. *Can we lose our salvation?*

# 2 Our goal

*Let us run with perseverance the race
marked out for us. (Hebrews 12:1)*

*Your life is short, your duties many, your assistance
great, and your reward sure; therefore, faint not, hold
on and hold up, in ways of well-doing, and heaven
shall make amends for all. (Thomas Brooks)*

It was just after my sixtieth birthday that my mother-in-law, who was then ninety-two, came to live with us. Her sight had deteriorated over the previous ten years, she had been registered blind and she was no longer able to look after herself. As I assumed the role of carer, my husband believed it to be essential that I had some time to myself. To ensure that this became a reality, he bought me a year's membership at our local gym. Initially I wondered whether he was my friend or foe! It was only when I began to exercise that I realized just how much healthier I felt all round, and it soon became quite obvious to me how out of shape I had become.

As we look back at photographs or images of ourselves and others through the years, we may be quite shocked at the change we notice—a change which is not always for the better! The truth is that few people stay the same shape throughout the course of their lives. We do not remain static! Exercise is needed if our bodies are not to get seriously out of shape.

And the same is true for us spiritually. Paul tells Timothy, 'Train yourself to be godly. For physical training is of some value, but godliness has value for all things, holding promise for both the present life and the life to come' (1 Timothy 4:7b–8). However great the benefits of physical exercise, they do not begin to compare with the spiritual benefits that flow from godliness: 'This is [our] proper occupation . . . you will do that which is of the highest importance, if you devote yourself, with all your zeal, and all your ability, to godliness alone . . . It is the beginning, the middle, and the end, of Christian life.'[1]

This is something of which we need to be reminded in this age when physical training and exercise has become, for some, not merely an aspect of proper care of the bodies God has given us, but a veritable obsession. Whether you are into physical training or are one of those who is not that concerned about it (the thought of regular exercise might even terrify you!), the fact of the matter is that it is essential for all Christians to *train themselves to be godly*.

### SPIRITUAL EXPECTATIONS

When I started at the fitness club, the personal trainer asked me, 'What are your goals? And what do you realistically hope to achieve within the next twelve months?' Do we have as much foresight spiritually? Have we a fitness programme set up to help us grow in grace? From the verses quoted above from 1 Timothy we see that such training has a value for '*all* things': that is, for everything our lives encompass, and not just for the here and now: '*holding promise for both the present life and the life to come*'.[2] These 'all things' will benefit us right into eternity: therefore, we need to take them seriously. What are my goals as a Christian? Have I spiritual expectations for my growth and development as a child of God? We never remain the same 'shape' as Christians: we either go forward or, as is all too often the case, we slip back. And sadly, at times, we do not even notice our lack of spiritual energy; we just get used to plodding along. If we compare ourselves with others around us, we may even regard ourselves as being in quite good shape. It is only when our gauge is placed against the Saviour, with His matchless righteousness, that our Christian physique looks way below average!

**SPIRITUAL WELL-BEING**

So let us take stock of ourselves. What do we care about most in our lives? Is it merely our bodies? By that I do not just mean what our bodies look like when we exit the gym, but the excessive amount of time we spend preening ourselves. Our greater concern should be for our spiritual well-being. We might know that in our heads, but do we make it essential to our living? We can gain much by taking seriously this injunction to live godly lives which will profit us in 'all things', not just in things temporal. Let us not leave aims and aspirations in the gym; rather let us incorporate them into our lives. Someone once said, 'Aim for the stars, and you may hit the chimney!' In other words, if reality so often falls far short of aspiration, what will happen if we have no goals or godly ambitions? May it be our goal *to have an aim*; we have but one life, and we need it to count for God. Robert Murray M'Cheyne, a godly Scottish preacher who died when he was only twenty-nine years old, once wrote to a fellow preacher: 'It is not great talents God blesses so much as great likeness to Jesus. A holy minister is an awful [= awesome!] weapon in the hand of God.'[3] M'Cheyne set spiritual goals for himself: what could be a more appropriate prayer than his oft-repeated request that God would make him *as holy as a saved sinner could be*? This, surely, was part of the 'secret' that lay behind his extraordinary and spiritually effective life, a life lived in such communion with God that Dr Candlish said of him, 'I can't understand M'Cheyne: grace seems to be natural to him.'[4]

What M'Cheyne was himself, and what he urged on others in the nineteenth century, Kevin de Young presses on us in the twenty-first century: 'If we are to be passionate in our pursuit of personal holiness, the first thing we must establish is that holiness is possible. It sounds humble to say, "I cannot obey God for one nanosecond in my life," but it's not true.'[5] He refers to people like Zechariah and Elizabeth, both of whom were righteous before God (Luke 1:6), and Job, who was a blameless and upright man (Job 1:8). It would appear from even just these examples cited by de Young— and there are many more—that holiness is a possibility, as well as a necessity, for God's people. But it does not come automatically: as Hebrews 12:14 informs us, we must 'make every effort . . . to be holy'. So although God, in His grace, has already 'given us everything that we need for a godly life' (2 Peter 1:3), this does not mean that we do not need to put in effort. Quite the contrary! It is precisely because God has given us everything for a godly life that we must make every effort to advance: 'For this very reason, make every effort to add to your faith . . .' (2 Peter 1:5). So much exercise is needed!

De Young goes on to say,

If the possibility of holiness is so plain in the Bible, why do we find it so hard to believe? Probably the biggest reason is because we equate obedience with perfection . . . God doesn't expect us to be the best in everything in order to be free from paralyzing guilt . . . It's our Christ-like character that counts . . . God is pleased through Christ to accept our sincere obedience, although it contains many weaknesses and imperfections.[6]

## SPIRITUAL GROWTH

If we are spiritually healthy, it should surely be our goal and desire to be as godly as a 'saved sinner can be': 'Godliness[7] has value for *all* things', whereas physical training has only *some* value and is temporary: it benefits us only as long as we live. As human beings we grow physically, mentally and emotionally. Such growth is, of course, not inevitable: food, exercise, rest, study, social interaction and a myriad other things play their part in human development. It is always sad when growth becomes stunted in any of these areas. How sad, too, when a Christian becomes stunted in his or her spiritual growth! But without feeding on God's Word, spending time in prayer, fellowshipping and serving Him on a daily basis, growth cannot take place and we will become underdeveloped. True, it is not these things that cause growth: it is God Himself who does this. This is why Jesus prayed for his disciples, 'Sanctify them by the truth' (John 17:17). Only God could sanctify them, and only God can sanctify us. But God uses *means*— what Christians used to call 'the means of grace'. Have we considered that we may be stunted in our spiritual growth? That we may be going through the motions, as it were, to keep up appearances before others, but that inwardly our spiritual life has shrivelled and dried up?

John Newton, that wonderful man of God who was converted to faith in Christ from a terrible life as the blaspheming captain of a slave-trading ship, knew that he owed everything to God's grace. And so today we joyfully sing his great hymn 'Amazing Grace'. One of the surest signs of spiritual growth is that we increasingly appreciate how amazing God's grace truly is. Newton never ceased to be amazed by it. He was a man who truly grew 'in the grace and knowledge of our Lord and Saviour Jesus Christ' (2 Peter 3:18). But—and this is one of the great paradoxes of the Christian life—those who grow most have the lowliest view of themselves. Does this mean that it is impossible to discern growth? Does it mean that it is something which only God and others can see? Well, yes, and no. For Newton could famously say, 'I am not what I shall be; I am not what I wish to be. But I thank God that I am not what I was and, by the grace of God, I am what I am.'[8]

We too should be able to say as each year goes by, 'I may not be as I would like to be, but I know I am going forward, not slipping back. I am taking daily nourishment and exercise to ensure I grow.' Let us then take a peep into the spiritual gym and make it our aim and practice to be more energetic and disciplined in our pursuit of godliness.[9]

. . . that the body of Christ may be built up until
we . . . become mature. (Ephesians 4:12b–13)

## Food for thought

1. *Do you devise 'outlets' for your over-burdened lifestyle? Realistically, what could these outlets be? Think of things that could be done on a limited budget and with little free time.*

2. *Do you have spiritual aims and goals? Have you ever set yourself spiritual goals?*

3. *Do you feel encouraged or deflated as you look over the past year? Have you grown in grace, stayed static or perhaps regressed?*

### Notes

1  Calvin, *Calvin's Calvinism*, pp. 108–109.

2  All emphasis in Scripture quotes has been added.

3  Bonar, *Memoirs and Remains*, p. 16.

4  Bonar, *Reminiscences*, p. 10.

5  De Young, *Hole in Our Holiness*, p. 65.

6  Ibid., p. 67.

7  See Appendix 1, 'What Is Godliness?'

8  John Newton, as quoted in *The Christian Pioneer* (1856), edited by Joseph Foulkes Winks, p. 84. Also in *The Christian Spectator*, vol. 3 (1821), p. 186. 'I am not what I ought to be—ah, how imperfect and deficient! I am not what I wish to be—I abhor what is evil, and I would cleave to what is good! I am not what I hope to be—soon, soon shall I put off mortality, and with mortality all sin and imperfection. Yet, though I am not what I ought to be, nor what I wish to be, nor what I hope to be, I can truly say, I am not the man I wish to be, and I am not the man I hope to be, but by the grace of God, I am not the man I used to be.' (Often paraphrased as the above.)

9  See Appendix 2, 'The Marks of Godliness'.

# 3 God's goal

*For those God foreknew he also predestined to be
conformed to the image of his Son. (Romans 8:29)*

*Blessed and holy are Christ's people! From sorrow, cross, and
conflict they are not saved; but they are 'saved from sin' for
evermore. They are cleansed from guilt by Christ's blood.
They are made meet for heaven by Christ's Spirit. This is
salvation! He who cleaves to sin is not yet saved. (J. C. Ryle)*

We must be concerned that *our* ultimate goal is the same as *God's* ultimate goal for us. Christ's purpose is one day to present us 'without stain or wrinkle or any other blemish' (Ephesians 5:27b), making us radiant. That means a lot of ground work, a lot of exercise, is required to make us spiritually flawless. Timothy Lane and Paul David Tripp say,

What is the goal of this change? It is more than a better
marriage, well-adjusted children, professional success or
freedom from a few nagging sins. *God's goal* is that we would
actually become like Him . . . His goal is to free us from our
slavery to sin, our bondage to sin, our bondage to self, and our
functional idolatry, so that we actually take on His character.[1]

## STOP SNACKING

We can, however, be satisfied with less than the best. We can become indolent and ill-disciplined.

Very closely aligned with physical exercise is diet, which

has a big effect on our well-being. A woman I see regularly at the gym spends three hours a day on her workout but is still overweight and has not changed her shape during the last year. I can only conclude that she is not treating her intake as seriously as her output! The problem begins when we start eating just what we like, not checking whether it will be to our benefit or whether it is actually doing us harm. There is also a tendency in us to eat just when we like. We need to have regular meals—and to stop snacking. However, we usually become serious with regard to our diet when we feel sick, off our food or unable to digest anything; that is usually an indication that, physically, things are not right. Perhaps we have eaten something that does not agree with us, picked up a bug or contracted some illness. When this happens, we do not sit in a corner and expect things to right themselves; we take some action, even if it is only to sip some water! Being unwell may cause us to become languid, feeling not at all like ourselves.

For some, however, even the most mundane and common ailments can lead them to overreact and imagine the worst, envisaging themselves at death's door! This is hypochondria.

**STOP BEING CAVALIER**

Sadly, in the spiritual realm, our problem is often the exact opposite. Far from suffering from spiritual hypochondria, we may 'under-react', feeling little concern or adopting a cavalier attitude towards symptoms that indicate all is not well. Perhaps we have little appetite to read God's Word, or maybe the Word of God figures nowhere in our lives. A spiritual lethargy and languor descends upon us so that real prayer slips by the wayside too. Do we at this point desire to address the problem? Or do we rather start justifying to ourselves the reasons why we are as we are?

I am not talking about those times when the pressures we are under may make it impossible for us to have any time to spend alone with God. But, those times aside, we need to remind ourselves that we cannot expect to grow spiritually without spiritual food. Are we in the habit of reading the Word of God regularly? And, if we have no real appetite for God's Word, are we asking the Lord to show us why this is so, and to whet our spiritual appetite? He is willing to help us, but we have to ask. We must go to the heavenly Physician!

### PHYSICAL OR SPIRITUAL?

The symptoms of a physical illness sometimes come upon us suddenly, but at other times there is a more gradual awareness that something is not right. And the same can hold true in our spiritual lives. I am not thinking of those times when Christians pass through what might be called 'spiritual depression' or 'desertion': such experiences can be very dark indeed, and yet are *not* necessarily an indication that the individual believer has lost his or her way. The causes of such things can be varied. It may be a time of satanic onslaught; there may be physical factors; or the Lord may withdraw, for a season, the sense of His presence so that the Christian will learn to walk more by faith, lean more upon the Lord and plead the promises of His Word. On such occasions the believer may well need help from a true shepherd of the soul, and sometimes medical help.

### SPIRITUAL ANAEMIA

However, my concern is not with such times, but rather with our tendency to laxity or lassitude. We may become spiritually anaemic as a result of failing to take 'the iron rations for our soul'. We feed ourselves with the equivalent of spiritual candyfloss rather than with those things which will truly build us up spiritually, such as the milk and then, as we mature, the strong meat of God's Word. Or it may be that we have nurtured a sin which has the effect of draining us of spiritual energy.

Some years ago, I gradually became conscious of a measure of breathlessness. It reached the point where I was panting even when lying in bed! I did not take it very seriously, but my husband suggested I should see my doctor. I was still not convinced but mentioned it casually to a Christian GP in my church. She said that I should definitely see my doctor. The result? I was breathless because I had become anaemic; but the anaemia was related to something else, and the upshot was that I had to undergo surgery. A course of iron supplements would have done me no good if the underlying problem had not been addressed. Similarly, a loss of spiritual energy *may* be the result of some sin draining away the vital energies of our spiritual life. If that is so, no amount of Bible reading, listening to sermons or attending conferences will address the problem: the sin must be dealt with. In other words, we must be doers as well as hearers of God's Word, as James says (James 1:22). Why is it that some never face up to the cause of spiritual declension? Might it be that it is easier to ignore the truth rather than look it in the eye and do something about it? Is this not, in fact, what James goes on to urge upon us (James

1:23–25)? We are to look at ourselves in the mirror, and not turn away and the next moment forget what we have seen; we must confront our sin, deal with it, and concentrate on God. '"The practice of godliness is an exercise or discipline that focuses upon God . . ." So often we try to develop Christian character and conduct without taking time to develop God-centered devotion. We try to please God without taking the time to walk with Him and develop a relationship with Him. This is impossible to do.'[2]

## SPIRITUAL BALANCE

We must, of course, guard against lopsidedness. It would be ridiculous for a man to spend hours in the gym building up his biceps, pectoral muscles or all the muscles of his upper torso, only to find that his legs were too weak and spindly to carry him! Or for a woman to lose so much weight that a gust of wind might blow her over! Balance is what is needed. There is an all-roundedness to the Christian character: our reading of God's Word and communing with Him in prayer should produce a 'roundedness' in our Christian lives that is displayed in the way we serve the Lord in the family, in the church, in the workplace and in society at large. It is possible for the believer to lose sight of this fact and make an *end* of those things which God has given to us as a *means* to the end or goal that He has for us. A Christian lady once told me that her unconverted husband was always complaining that the house was untidy. The reason why she never had time to clean the home was, as her husband complained, 'You've always got your head stuck in *that book*,' meaning the Bible.

HIS TREASURED POSSESSION

She was to be commended for her desire and diligence, but certainly not for her imbalance.

## RELATIONSHIP, NOT ACHIEVEMENT

We constantly need to remind ourselves that the Lord gives to us because He loves us, and He has given us His Word so that we can read it and, through it, come to know *Him* better and grow to be more and more like Him. He has not given us the Bible so that it might gather dust on a shelf, nor as an excuse for us to neglect other important duties: balance with health checks is vitally important. One fears that the former, rather than the latter, is the danger we face today. We are to love God's Word, but never use it as an excuse for indolence. Regular, systematic reading of the Scriptures is paramount. However, there may be times when a well-ordered and disciplined study of God's Word is not possible.

I found myself in such a situation when training to be a teacher many years ago. I was on placement for my final teaching practice and was fortunate to be lodging with a lovely, godly Christian family. I faced a very hard and intensive eight weeks of work and preparation each day. I was often up very early in the morning for Bible reading and prayer, because it was the only time I could slot in for personal study. Usually I was still preparing my lessons till way past midnight. As the weeks rolled by, I became more and more exhausted. One morning, when I quietly crept down to the lounge to have my devotions, I was so tired that I could not even remember the words of the Lord's Prayer, let alone my own weary prayers. Fortunately for me, I had not been quiet enough: my 'house mother' heard me pass her bedroom door and followed me downstairs a short time later. There she found me crying. She simply took me in her arms and said, 'The Lord knows all about your need; just learn to lean on Him. He isn't a taskmaster. The Lord knows about all the work you are having to do; He doesn't drive His lambs. He will carry you in His arms when you are in need.'

At times we can all feel as I did—the days can be so busy and long—but God knows all about our situations. He is always there for us to look to, and we need to learn to 'lean hard' on Him.[3] What a timely word that was for me! I had forgotten that it is all about *relationship*, not *achievement*. If we mistake the two we will lose out. We need to assess ourselves and our circumstances. We can go on blindly without gauging our spiritual needs. This will be to our loss. God's desire and goal for us is *Himself*: not a shadow or some plastic counterfeit, but reality! 'God is in the process of preparing us for heaven, to dwell with Him for eternity. So He desires that we grow both in holiness and godliness. He wants us to be like Him.[4]

### SPIRITUAL VIGOUR

As we study the whole subject of growth in godliness, we shall look in the following chapters at how we can help ourselves, by God's grace and His Spirit, to keep spiritual vigour and maintain a healthy spirit, continually growing in our knowledge of God, but remembering also to keep a right balance in our lives. Do we not see this wonderfully displayed and exemplified in the life of our Lord Jesus Christ? Everything was 'in place' in His life; nothing was 'out of place'. He is to be the pattern for our lives, and God's goal is for us to be conformed to His likeness. May this be our goal too!

I keep asking that the God of our Lord Jesus Christ, the glorious Father, may give you the Spirit of wisdom and revelation, so that you may know him better. (Ephesians 1:17)

## Food for thought

1. *Are you daily conscious of God's goal for you: 'to free us from our slavery to sin, our bondage to sin, our bondage to self, and our functional idolatry, so that we actually take on His character' (Lane and Tripp)?*

2. *Are you disciplining yourself to pray and read God's Word regularly?*

3. *Do you realize that God's greatest desire for you is that you should have a relationship with Him, not that you should just 'perform'?*

### Notes

1   Lane and Tripp, *Change Is Possible*, p. 15.

2   Bridges, *Practice of Godliness*, p. 18.

3   See the poem 'Lean Hard' in Appendix 3.

4   Bridges, *Practice of Godliness*, p. 22.

# 4 Strong as death: exercising love

*This love of which I speak is slow to lose patience—it looks
for a way of being constructive. It is not possessive: it is neither
anxious to impress nor does it cherish inflated ideas of its own
importance. Love has good manners and does not pursue selfish
advantage. It is not touchy. It does not keep account of evil or
gloat over the wickedness of other people. On the contrary,
it is glad with all good men when truth prevails. Love knows
no limit to its endurance, no end to its trust, no fading of its
hope; it can outlast anything. It is, in fact, the one thing that
still stands when all else has fallen. (1 Corinthians 13:4–8a)[1]*

*If we have got the love of God shed abroad in our hearts,
we will show it in our lives. We will not have to go up
and down the earth proclaiming it. We will show it
in everything we say or do. (Dwight L. Moody)*

L ove, the Bible tells us, is the greatest virtue. In the
Song of Songs love is described in this way:

Love is as strong as death,
   its jealousy unyielding as the grave.
It burns like blazing fire,
   like a mighty flame.
Many waters cannot quench love;
   rivers cannot sweep it away.
If one were to give
   all the wealth of one's house for love,
   it would be utterly scorned.
(Song of Songs 8:6b–7)

What a description of love! Who would not want a love like that? This is different from the insipid love that is portrayed by Hollywood or by the world in which we live. It is certainly not a love we can possess in and of ourselves; it is a love that can only be possessed by those whom God possesses. Jonathan Edwards said,

All the fruits of the Spirit which we are to lay weight upon as evidential of grace, are summed up in charity, or Christian love, because this is the sum of all grace. And the only way, therefore, in which any can know their good estate, is by discerning the exercises of this divine charity in their hearts; for without charity, let men have what gifts you please, they are nothing.[2]

## WHOM DO WE IMITATE?

We are commanded to love God, to love our brothers and sisters, to love our enemies—whether in or out of the church!—and to exercise that love in any and every situation. Augustine demonstrates an all-encompassing view of love when he answers the question 'What does love look like?': 'It has the hands to help others. It has the feet to hasten to the poor and needy. It has the eyes to see misery and want. It has the ears to hear the sighs and sorrows of men. That is what love looks like.'[3]

This is what our Saviour looks like! And this is what we should look like! We are told to imitate, and love, as Christ loved us: 'Follow God's example . . . and live a life of love, just as Christ loved us' (Ephesians 5:1-2). We are commanded to 'keep [ourselves] in God's love' (Jude 21). John tells us, 'Whoever lives in love lives in God, and God in them . . . We love because he first loved us' (1 John

4:16a, 19). Whether we are encouraged to imitate Christ or commanded to love as God loves, any statement we find in the Bible will find us wanting. We can only hope to know this love as it is shed abroad in our hearts by the Holy Spirit. 'As God's chosen people, holy and dearly loved, clothe yourselves with compassion, kindness, humility, gentleness and patience . . . And over all these virtues put on love, which binds them all together in perfect unity' (Colossians 3:12, 14). There are many passages of Scripture that emphasize the virtue of love and the importance of exhibiting this grace in our lives, so it behoves us to be constantly asking God to endow us with His Spirit, that we might be enabled to love as He loves.

### LOVE AS HE LOVES

We cannot love like God unless God enables us to. Do we wonder why we cannot love that awkward/annoying/ difficult/trying person? Are we endeavouring to love him or her in our own strength? If so, we will surely fail. We need to come to God and ask Him for help to grow in love towards that man or woman.

Growth is one of the *evidences* of life; and spiritual growth is evidenced as we grow in love towards God and towards one another. Love for God is authentic when it leads to, or overflows in, love for our fellow Christian. 'For whoever does not love their brother and sister, whom they have seen, cannot love God, whom they have not seen. And he has given us this command: anyone who loves God must also love their brother and sister' (1 John 4:20b–21). So if there is a brother or sister whom we do not love, we are not obeying God; we are sinning. But perhaps we excuse ourselves by saying, 'Well, I just don't get on with him/her'; or 'He/she is so difficult and provocative'; or even 'He/she is downright odd.' That person, whether or not we regard him or her as our type or as 'odd', is still our brother or sister! We usually do not give up on our own flesh and blood; how much more, then, should we love and persevere with those for whom Christ died! C. H. Spurgeon speaks on the subject of love and forgiveness in his inimical way:

I wish, brothers and sisters, that we could all imitate the pearl oyster. A harmful particle intrudes itself into its shell, and this vexes and grieves it. It cannot eject the evil, and what does it do but *cover* it with a precious substance extracted out of its own life, by which it turns the intruder into a pearl. Oh, that we could do so with the provocations we receive from our fellow Christians, so that pearls of patience, gentleness, longsuffering, and forgiveness might be created within us by what otherwise would have harmed us.[4]

I well remember, sometime after getting married, being in a church where a young woman shared with me that she really disliked a Christian sister of about the same age in the church, finding her very difficult to get on with. This proved a bit of a problem because, apart from myself, she and the woman she disliked were the only young women in the church! I asked her how often she prayed for this 'sister'. It appeared from her response that she had prayed about the circumstance, but not for the woman in question. I challenged her to pray not only for the situation but also for the woman. I had to move away from the area and the church soon after because of my husband's work, but when I was next in the district

I enquired about her difficulty. She shared that it had been wonderfully resolved: she had become the best of friends with the woman she had not found easy. But now she had a different 'problem': her friend was having to relocate because of her work, and she now found herself heart-broken! D. L. Moody explains, 'It may not be an easy thing to live in sweet fellowship with all those with whom we come in contact; but that is what the grace of God is given to us for.[5]

## RIPPLES IN A POND

And this love can conquer our prejudices or dislike of people. Growth in love is a very beautiful thing: for us to witness in others, and for others to see in us. To love can bring great joy to those we love as well as to our own hearts. But the greater joy and pleasure is brought to the God of love, who delights to see His children bear with one another and display 'the family likeness'. Augustine of Hippo said, 'Since love grows within you, so beauty grows. For love is the beauty of the soul.'[6] Loving God to the uttermost and pleasing Him should be our souls' desire. Loving others, particularly those we do not find easy to love, is an expression of our love for God. We should guard our hearts with great diligence. The root cause of our failure to love may be our impoverished love for God. Maurice Roberts says,

Backsliding in the soul always begins with a decline in our love for the Saviour Himself. We grow cold towards the One who died for us . . . Perhaps the greatest need as Christians is to rise above the habitual coolness with which we treat the love of Christ. If Jesus Christ is God and died for me, as a great missionary once said, then no sacrifice is too great for me to make for Him. Let every believer say the same.[7]

Love for God is essential. It keeps the flame of love towards others burning brightly. Just as a pebble dropped into a pond sends out ripples, so this God-given love can spread out and touch others. The love of God in our hearts can be like an overflowing fountain that reaches and refreshes all those with whom we have to do: 'May the Lord make your love increase and overflow for each other and for everyone else' (1 Thessalonians 3:12). To love God and others is not an option: 'If you really keep the royal law found in Scripture, "Love your neighbour as yourself," you are doing right' (James 2:8). Sadly, our churches do not always exhibit this wonderful essential quality of love for Christ and His people. They should be havens of love, where those battered by this world's storms can find refuge. If we are not demonstrating this kind of love, what a lost opportunity of witness to a loveless world!

I pray that out of his glorious riches he may strengthen you with power through his Spirit in your inner being, so that Christ may dwell in your hearts through faith. And I pray that you, being rooted and established in love, may have power, together with all the Lord's holy people, to grasp how wide and long and high and deep is the love of Christ, and to know this love that surpasses knowledge—that you may be filled to the measure of all the fullness of God. (Ephesians 3:16–19)

## Food for thought

1. *Are you trying to love in your own strength?*

2. *Is there someone in your church you find difficult? How can you possibly love him or her?*
3. *Do you 'give up' on brothers and sisters?*
4. *If your church is not a 'haven of love', how can you help to make it so?*

**Notes**

**1** J. B. Phillips New Testament (1972).

**2** Edwards, *Christian Love and Its Fruits*, p. 22.

**3** Augustine of Hippo, *Confessions*, quoted at BrainyQuote, https://www.brainyquote.com/quotes/saint_augustine_148553.

**4** '1617. Love's Labours, by Charles H. Spurgeon', point 18, quoted at Answers in Genesis, https://answersingenesis.org/education/spurgeon-sermons/1617-loves-labours/.

**5** Moody, *Prevailing Prayer*, ch. 6, 'Forgiveness', p 61.

**6** Augustine of Hippo, quoted at BrainyQuote, https://www.brainyquote.com/quotes/saint_augustine_385078.

**7** Roberts, *Great God of Wonders*, pp. 149–150. The 'great missionary' was C. T. Studd.

# 5 Holding tightly: developing faith

*The life I now live in the body, I live by faith in the Son of God, who loved me and gave himself for me. (Galatians 2:20b)*

*It is the nature of faith to believe God upon His bare word . . . It will not be, saith sense; it cannot be, saith reason; it both can and will be, saith faith, for I have a promise. (John Trapp)*

Faith is another area in which we must grow or decline. The Bible's definition of faith is found in Hebrews 11:1: it is having 'confidence in what we hope for and assurance about what we do not see'. This means that we are confident that God created the universe (past) and will fulfil His promises for the as-yet-unseen future. This is no blind faith but is a trust in God's proven faithfulness. I remember, as a young Christian, looking at the Bible of an elderly saint. I asked her why she had written 'T. P.' numerous times in the margin of many of its pages. She simply said, 'Oh, that stands for "tried and proved"—God is so faithful to His promises.' And so He is! Faith is *believing* in God and *trusting* Him. However, we need to distinguish between the believing which is just believing what we want to believe, and believing in that which God has promised in His Word.

## NOT WISHFUL THINKING

I recall that, when my husband and I were contemplating

moving to our first church, I was convinced that God was going to supply us with a beautiful five-bedroomed, three-storey house, right opposite where we were meeting as a church. We had no money, but I knew that that was no problem for God. When I shared this with my husband, my faith was dismantled as wishful thinking when he said, 'And where in Scripture does God promise us a five-bedroomed, three-storey house?' As it turned out, a lovely Christian lady ended up in my 'dream' home, and we moved to a much smaller house in the town. We had wonderful opportunities to serve God there where He had placed us. So faith is not wishful thinking, but knowing what God's will is for us. Arthur W. Pink puts it very tellingly:

The prevailing idea seems to be, that I come to God and ask Him for something that I want, and that I expect Him to give me that which I have asked. But this is a most dishonoring and degrading conception. The popular belief reduces God to a servant, our servant: doing our bidding, performing our pleasure, granting our desires. No, prayer is a coming to God, telling Him my need, committing my way unto the Lord, and leaving Him to deal with it as seemeth Him best.[1]

## A SPECIFIC GIFT

Now there is a specific gift of faith that God gives to some people and which must be distinguished from the gift of saving faith that God gives to all His children. I could not have had that gift of faith, or I would not have entertained doubt or mistrusted my judgement when my husband challenged me. In 1 Corinthians 12:8a, 9a, Paul writes, 'To one there is given . . . faith.' Here faith is being referred to as a special gift, so it cannot be the faith we are *all* called to exercise. A great example of someone who had this kind of faith was George Müller, although he never claimed that he had such a special gift of faith: he said he just 'believed' and 'trusted' his heavenly Father.[2] There are many examples of this absolute trust which he exhibited in his daily walk with God. The following excerpt is but one example from the many entries in George Müller's diary:

The children are dressed and ready for school. But there is no food for them to eat,' the housemother of the orphanage informed George Mueller. George asked her to take the 300 children into the dining room and have them sit at the tables. He thanked God for the food and waited. George knew God would provide food for the children as he always did. Within minutes, a baker knocked on the door. 'Mr. Mueller,' he said, 'last night I could not sleep. Somehow, I knew that you would need bread this morning. I got up and baked three batches for you. I will bring it in.'

Soon, there was another knock at the door. It was the milkman. His cart had broken down in front of the orphanage. The milk would spoil by the time the wheel was fixed. He asked George if he could use some free milk. George smiled as the milkman brought in ten large cans of milk. It was just enough for the 300 thirsty children.[3]

It was this sort of giving and receiving, in smaller and larger amounts, day by day, month by month, and year by year, that made up the material fabric of Müller's life for sixty-nine years! He never canvassed for money for his homes or schools. God never failed him, or those under his care, and George Müller never distrusted his Saviour: he simply went to his heavenly Father with all the stresses and strains which accompanied the running of an orphanage of some thousands of children. And Müller gave God all the praise and glory for His abundant provision.

## REST IN HIM

So often, we come to some problem or difficulty in our lives and we pray, and then we anxiously thrash about for ways in which we think God might answer our prayers. That is what some call 'half trust'. We may certainly believe that God is going to answer our prayers, but frequently we act as though we think that the Lord needs a foreman or forewoman to help Him with the task, and we can almost get to the point where we are suggesting to Him how best He can answer our prayers. Proverbs 3:5 says, 'Trust in the LORD with all your heart and lean not on your own understanding.' We are not told *not* to use our understanding, but that we must not *lean* on it. We must learn to lean on the Lord. To believe God will act, even when circumstances seem to suggest He has forgotten, is what exercising faith is all about.

We are to have faith in God's ability and in His great power to be 'able to do immeasurably more than all we ask or imagine' (Ephesians 3:20a). We must learn to leave our problems with the Lord and wait patiently to see how He chooses to resolve them. This is but one way of ensuring that our 'faith is growing more and more' (2 Thessalonians 1:3). We learn to exercise our weak faith: 'Therefore, strengthen your feeble arms and weak knees' (Hebrews 12:12); and waiting on God's activity is one way of doing so. May we make every effort to exercise our faith in every situation in which we find ourselves. We should learn to view every obstacle in our path, or every trial in our way, as an opportunity to trust God and see Him at work in our lives, helping us to grow 'more and more'.

As a very young Christian I read the poem 'One Day' by Mary Butterfield (see Appendix 4) which helped me view difficulties in a very different light. This poem speaks of 'weights' that overwhelm us and which can often make us feel crushed. But the poem reminds us that God has a different purpose in mind in our trials: He intends them to be like wings that will encourage us to fly to Him. We are, in faith, 'to mount up with wings as eagles' (Isaiah 40:31, KJV). Often, instead of exercising faith, we want to *see* where we are going and what God is doing, rather than resting in Him, waiting for His time and following His cue. There is an unwillingness, on our part, for the Lord to conceal the next step from us. In so doing, we can come close to trying to write God's agenda for Him.

When will we ever just let God sort things out for us? When will we ever learn that He can be trusted perfectly? The Scriptures encourage us to be spiritually alert and to keep our eyes on the pathway in front of us. But sometimes we cannot see ahead, and the way is dim. At such times we must be willing to press on with doing what God commands and to cling to Him, just as a child holds tightly onto its parent's hand in the dark. The wonderful thing is that His hold of us is always more sure than is ours of Him.

In quietness and trust is your strength. (Isaiah 30:15b)

## Food for thought

   1. *Do you trust God's 'proven faithfulness'? How do past answers to prayer help us to grow in faith?*

2. *How can we discern whether or not our prayers are just wishful thinking?*

3. *Are you ever unwittingly God's foreman or forewoman? If so, how can you prevent this from happening?*

4. *How should we view the problems and difficulties that thread our path?*

**Notes**

1   Pink, *Sovereignty of God*, p. 107.

2   Müller, *Autobiography*, pp. 173–177.

3   'George Mueller, Orphanages Built by Prayer', Christianity.com, 16 July 2010, http://www.christianity.com/church/church-history/church-history-for-kids/ george-mueller-orphanages-built-by-prayer-11634869.html. 'It should here be noted that, among the first givers, was a poor needlewoman who brought the surprising sum of one hundred pounds, the singular self-denial and whole hearted giving exhibited making this a peculiarly sacred offering and a token of God's favour. There was a felt significance in His choice of a poor sickly seamstress as His instrument for laying the foundations for this great work' (Pierson, *George Müller of Bristol*, p. 126).

# 6 Babes in a paddling pool: adding knowledge

*My goal is that they may be encouraged in heart ... in order that*
*they may know the mystery of God, namely, Christ, in whom*
*are hidden all the treasures of wisdom. (Colossians 2:2–3)*

*A man may be theologically knowing and*
*spiritually ignorant. (Stephen Charnock)*

It was Richard Cecil who said, 'The first step towards knowledge is to know that we are ignorant.' I do not know about you, but the place where I feel this more than anywhere else is in a well-stocked library: simply to consider the quantity of information contained in the vast array of books helps to impart a realistic view of just how ignorant one can be. The Internet can, alas, have the opposite effect: click with the mouse, and information is instantly available, but one is unable to see all that one has *not* accessed. Possibly one reason why many prefer the Internet to a library is because the Web can make you feel you know a lot, whereas the library cuts you down to size! Someone once said that ours is an age strong on information but weak on knowledge. But there is knowledge and there is knowledge: simply to fill one's head with facts for the sake of knowing things (or, worse, so that we can let others know that we know them!) is hardly the wisest use of time or energy and can be harmful to the soul. Spurgeon surely had it right when he wrote, 'Wisdom is . . . the right use of knowledge. To know is not to be wise. Many men know a great deal, and are all the more fools for what they know. There is no fool so great a fool as a knowing fool. But to know how to use knowledge is to have wisdom.[1]

The greatest knowledge is the knowledge of God. Unlike any other knowledge, this knowledge will never puff us up but will always humble us. This knowledge brings wisdom. It is *personal* knowledge: knowing a person, not simply knowing propositions about Him. Of course, we do need to know *about* Him; but it is possible to have such a knowledge without knowing God personally. God is infinite and His knowledge is infinite. Since everything else is finite, this means that God knows Himself fully and perfectly. We, of course, being finite and limited creatures, will never— and can never—know God in all His fullness. We are in an entirely different realm here from being in a well-stocked library: there is more of God to know than can be known from all the books in every library in the world, and from knowing perfectly every person in the world who has ever lived—literally, infinitely more! The knowledge of God is immense—an ocean—and we are like babes dipping our toes into a paddling pool! But the sooner we begin to know God, the greater will be our privilege of having a knowledge that is of eternal value. As Francis Schaeffer put it, 'While we do not have *exhaustive* knowledge, we can have *true* and unified knowledge.'[2] And, we might add, the knowledge of God we have is not only not exhaustive, but also it is not exhausting! Getting to know some things—even getting to know some people—can, on occasion, be exhausting. But knowing

God never exhausts or enervates; it always energizes and invigorates.

*The* chief aim of our lives should be to *know Christ*: to know Him experientially, rather than simply knowing *about* Him. Our knowledge *about* Him needs to work out in our experience, so that we glorify Him in our living. John Piper puts it thus: 'God is most glorified when you are most satisfied in Him. Knowledge about Him will not do. Work for Him will not do. We must have personal, vital fellowship with Him; otherwise, Christianity becomes a joyless burden.'[3]

### STRANGELY DISTANT AND COLD

We can all go through the motions of being a Christian: we can go to church and be diligent in attending the prayer meetings and the missionary meetings, yet be failing to nurture that vital relationship with God. As we look back on our lives, we may remember the excitement we once had when we discovered new things about God, and how important it was for us to meet with Him before we met with others each day. But what we 'once held dear'[4] and regularly put into practice may, alas, have long since been abandoned, and we may have become backslidden in heart—perhaps unknown to anyone but ourselves and God, or even, like the Ephesian Christians who had forsaken their first love (Revelation 2:4), unknown to ourselves as well. Our knowledge and enjoyment of God may have become strangely distant and cold, but God has a word for us in Jeremiah 29:12–13: 'Then you will call on me and come and pray to me, and I will listen to you. You will seek me and find me when you seek me with all your heart.' The situation need not continue. Let us call on Him with every fibre of our being, and let us know that wonderful renewal and reconciliation. Then, and only then, can we know Him better!

## NO CRINGING FEAR

When we know God in this way we will have the right fear of His Name: that is, we shall have a reverence, honour and awe when we approach Him. The late John Murray once wrote,

The fear of God is the soul of godliness . . . There is the dread or terror of the Lord and there is the fear of reverential awe. There is the fear that consists in being afraid; it elicits anguish and terror. There is the fear of reverence; it elicits confidence and love . . . The fear of God in which godliness consists is the fear which constrains adoration and love. It is the fear which consists in awe, reverence, honour, and worship, and all of these on the highest level of exercise.[5]

This is no cringing fear, but one that draws us in childlike confidence and faith to God as our heavenly Father. Proverbs 1:7 tells us, 'The fear of the LORD is the beginning of knowledge.' This 'knowledge' is not merely knowing *about* Him, but knowing Him in our innermost being. Philippians 3:10 says, 'I want to know Christ—yes, to know the power of his resurrection.' We cannot hope to know God more if we do not spend time with Him, studying His Word and meditating on what He has to say to us.

## GROWTH DOWNWARDS

The view that we thus have of the Lord in His sovereign rule of our lives demands that we bend not only our knees but our very lives before Him in deepest humility. As Proverbs 22:4

expresses it, 'Humility is the fear of the LORD.' Peter tells us in his first letter that we are to humble ourselves 'under God's mighty hand' (1 Peter 5:6). Is it because we have domesticated our God and have so small a view of Him that we no longer 'fear and bow' before Him? The Puritan writer Thomas Watson put it in his characteristically pithy way when he said that the right manner of growth 'is to grow less in one's own eyes'.[6] That great lover of the Puritans J. I. Packer underlined this when he wrote, 'Real spiritual growth is always growth downward, so to speak, into profound humility, which in healthy souls will become more and more apparent as they age.'[7]

As we get older, are we growing downwards by degrees? Are our souls in a healthier condition as each year passes? Are we walking *humbly* with our God? We cannot pick humility off a tree or shelf: it is not something we might buy on a farm or at a supermarket. Humility is *learned* in God's school. It is the result of knowing the truth about God in His greatness and holiness, and about ourselves in our smallness and sinfulness. John the Baptist expressed true humility when he said of Christ, 'He must become greater; I must become less' (John 3:30). The days in which we live do not help us to advance in this grace. While the world has never promoted the true knowledge of God which is the root of all true humility, former generations were at least characterized by a measure of modesty. Boastfulness and self-promotion were frowned upon: those whose lives were marked by such things were regarded, at best, as insufferable bores and, at worst, as appallingly ill-mannered. All that has changed, at least in the UK. *Self* is promoted endlessly in today's celebrity-obsessed culture. But this is entirely alien to God's kingdom. We should not feel at home in such an atmosphere, nor should our hearts provide soil in which such attitudes and behaviour can thrive. Sadly, however, we may find that we are nurturing the weed of pride: like bindweed, it can insidiously wrap itself around us, smothering and choking our spiritual life, and soon there is no distinction between us and the world. We cannot hope to grow in our knowledge of God unless our heads and hearts keep in step with the motto of God's school: 'Walk humbly with your God' (Micah 6:8b). We need to recapture and retain not just a picture but the reality of God's 'incomparably great power for us who believe' (Ephesians 1:19). When we see His power and know His presence, then we shall clothe ourselves with humility, rather than being wrapped in the convolvulus of pride. Pride is shrivelled in the presence of the Lord, as Isaiah discovered when he saw Him high and exalted in the temple (Isaiah 6:1–7).

## WHAT PLEASES THE LORD?

Ephesians 5:10 tells us that we are to 'find out what pleases the Lord'. In other words, we are to find out what makes Him happy. He must be first in our affections; we must know His thoughts, by being in daily contact with Him.

If I were to ask a woman, 'How is your husband?' and she replied, 'Well, I don't really know,' I would probably follow up with another question: 'When did you last see him?' I am sure I would be right to be concerned if the wife were to say, 'Well, I caught a glimpse of him last week'! Of course, there are periods in life when this kind of situation has to be so: for example, women whose husbands work in one of the emergency services might see little of them in the immediate aftermath of a major disaster; but these are exceptional situations. It would hardly be healthy if this were the norm. But is this how we know Christ: fleetingly, just catching a glimpse in the week, as it were, of 'the heavenly bridegroom'? Faith and knowledge go hand in hand: the more we know Him, the more we shall trust Him. True knowledge of God is a living and ongoing 'experience'.

### DO NOT PLAY TRUANT FROM GOD'S SCHOOL

We will not grow in the knowledge of God merely by sitting in an armchair and reading the latest volume on godliness, any more than sitting in an armchair and reading a book on body building will help us to develop muscle. The spiritual gym, like the physical one in the health club or recreation centre, does not operate like that. We must 'exercise [ourselves] unto godliness' (1 Timothy 4:7, KJV).

When my husband and I moved to the first church of which he became pastor, we found it very difficult in many ways. It was really akin to a pioneer work. The church was a small cause, and we could hardly survive on the stipend my husband was given. But it was sufficient to know that God had taken us there. Each week we regularly got on our knees asking Him to provide for our needs. He never failed us, although on many occasions the answer to our prayers came at the eleventh hour.

As it was too expensive to shop in the local town, because there were no large supermarkets at hand, once a month I would make a hundred-mile round trip with our daughter and son, aged three and one respectively. Off we three would go to the nearest sizeable town to shop in a hypermarket: an hour's journey there, shopping for two hours, and then an hour's drive home—longer, of course, if there were any traffic hold-ups!

On one particular occasion, the day before I was due to go on my next mammoth shopping trip, when I looked in the cupboards for that day's family meal I discovered I had very little to put before them. The Lord alone knew my need. It was He who had brought us to this place, and He had said in His Word that He would provide for us: He had also promised to provide our daily food. The Lord reminded me of these truths and promises, so I brought them to Him in prayer. He gave me His peace, enabling me to leave the outcome with Him. About an hour later, there was a knock at the front door. Opening it, I found a friend who owned a local shop standing on the doorstep. In his arms was a large tray of food. He asked, rather tentatively, whether or not I could possibly use any of the produce he had brought, as the freezers in his shop had suddenly broken down without any warning. You can imagine the joy in my heart at that moment! I did not share my predicament with him, but as I closed the door I comforted myself with the thought that my friend must surely have had his freezers insured for such an eventuality. I thanked the Lord, with a very full heart, that He had kept His word and provided for our needs. We only know experiences like these if we do not play truant from God's school!

How glad I was that God had directed me to His promises! I knew them, but that was not enough: I needed to plead them. At that crucial moment I had been reminded by the Lord of the things I knew of His character. Our life experiences are, of course, different for us all; but when the Lord demonstrates His unchanging goodness to us, it should not only draw from us a loving response of gratitude, but also provide us with an ever-deepening knowledge of our God and Saviour. Such demonstrations of His love are like stepping stones: the more we know of Christ by experience, the more we will learn to trust Him the next time we are exercised in our faith. Each experience of Him becomes like a pearl on a string. As time goes on, they become tangible proofs of His goodness, and through these very things we grow in our knowledge and experience of Him. John Newton expressed this point to perfection in one of his great hymns, 'Begone, Unbelief':

His love in time past forbids me to think
He'll leave me at last in sorrow to sink;
Each sweet Ebenezer I have in review
Confirms His good pleasure to see me quite through.

### THE VALUE OF THE REFINER'S FIRE

Are we getting stronger through each experience, or are our muscles becoming weaker? Are we limping along spiritually? In this sense we can have very feeble arms and weak knees, and we can really need that gym experience. Do we sometimes wonder why the Lord seems to send the same difficulty or trial more than once along our way? He loves us, but an inadequate theology may tell us otherwise. How often I have heard people say, 'God can't possibly love me because He has allowed . . . to happen.' Hebrews 12:5–6, 14 states, 'Do not make light of the Lord's discipline, and do not

lose heart when he rebukes you, because the Lord disciplines
the one he loves . . . without holiness no one will see the
Lord.' He may be allowing these very things to happen to
us precisely *because* He loves us and wants to strengthen us
as Christians in certain areas of our lives. Arthur Tappan
Pierson, commenting on Malachi 3:3, writes,

Our Father, who seeks to perfect His saints in holiness, knows
the value of the refiner's fire. It is with the most precious
metals that the metallurgist will take the greatest care. He
subjects the metal to a hot fire, for only the refiner's fire will
melt the metal, release the dross, and allow the remaining,
pure metal to take a new and perfect shape in the mold.
   A good refiner never leaves the crucible but . . . 'will sit'
down by it so the fire will not become even one degree
too hot and possibly harm the metal. And as soon as he
skims the last bit of dross from the surface and sees his face
reflected in the pure metal, he extinguishes the fire.[8]

Although no discipline is pleasant at the time, we need
to learn from such experiences and realize that God
will not leave us in the 'fire' one moment longer than is
necessary. Our knowledge of God will develop our frame
and character. The following wise words come from J. I.
Packer's book *Knowing God*:

[Our perplexing trials mean that] God in his wisdom means to
make something of us which we have not attained yet, and is
dealing with us accordingly. Perhaps he means to strengthen us
in patience, good humour, compassion, humility, or meekness,
by giving us some extra practice in exercising these graces under
especially difficult positions. Perhaps he has new lessons in self-
denial and self-distrust to teach us. Perhaps he wishes to break us
of complacency, or unreality, or undetected forms of pride and

conceit. Perhaps his purpose is simply to draw us closer to himself in conscious communion with him; for it is often the case, as all the saints know, that fellowship with the Father and the Son is most vivid and sweet, and Christian joy is greatest, when the cross is heaviest . . . Or perhaps God is preparing us for forms of service of which at present we have no inkling . . . 'He knows the way he taketh,' even if for the moment we do not. We may be frankly bewildered at things that happen to us, but God knows exactly what he is doing, and what he is after, in his handling of our affairs. Always, and in everything, he is wise; we shall see that hereafter, even where we never saw it here . . . Meanwhile, we ought not to hesitate to trust his wisdom, even when he leaves us in the dark.[9]

The Bible says of Abraham that he 'believed the LORD' (Genesis 15:6), and he certainly had his trials! And we also read that in spite of his many problems he was called 'God's friend' (James 2:23b). From this we see that God was demonstrating through those very difficulties how much He really loved him. Abraham, in the extremity of all his struggles, not only knew God, but was known by Him. May the same be true of us!

The wise prevail through great power,
   and those who have knowledge muster
their strength. (Proverbs 24:5)

## Food for thought

1. *What should be the chief aim of our lives?*
2. *What does the right knowledge of God produce in us?*
3. *How do faith and knowledge go hand in hand?*
4. *What is God seeking to build through the difficulties He brings across our paths?*

**HIS TREASURED POSSESSION**

## Notes

**1** '991. The Fourfold Treasure, by Charles H. Spurgeon', at Answers in Genesis, https://answersingenesis.org/education/spurgeon-sermons/991-the-fourfold-treasure/.

**2** Schaeffer, *Escape from Reason*, p. 29.

**3** Piper, *Desiring God* (1996), p. 175.

**4** From the song by Graham Kendrick, 'Knowing You (All I Once Held Dear)' (1993).

**5** Murray, *Principles of Conduct*, pp. 229, 233, 236. Albert N. Martin writes, '"The fear of God is the soul of godliness." These opening words of Professor Murray's chapter on this theme are like a bucket of ice water thrown into one's face in a day of cozy, comfortable, man-centered and casual Christianity. However they are true words. In this booklet Prof. Murray convincingly defines the fear of God and then demonstrates from the Old and New Testaments how central it is to any biblically framed experience of the Christian life. May God be pleased to use these pages to move many to rethink this central theme of the Word of God.' Endorsement by Al Martin of John Murray, *The Fear of God: The Soul of Godliness*, booklet with material taken from Murray, *Principles of Conduct*. Quoted at Solid Ground Christian Books, http://www.solid-ground-books.com/detail_954.asp.

**6** Watson, *Body of Divinity*, p. 273.

**7** Packer, *Finishing Our Course with Joy*, p. 95.

**8** Quoted in Cowman, *Streams in the Desert*, for October 29. Cowman then quotes James Grey's poem 'The Refiner': see Appendix 5.

**9** Packer, *Knowing God*, pp. 104–105.

# 7 No dirty tools: promoting holiness

*God disciplines us for our good, in order that we may share in his holiness. (Hebrews 12:10b)*

*There is nothing destroyed by sanctification, but that which would destroy us. (William Jenkyn)*

We are called to be holy as God is holy, but what does holiness really mean? R. C. Sproul, in his book *The Holiness of God*, explains:

The primary meaning of holy is 'separate'. It comes from an ancient word that meant 'to cut', or 'to separate'. Perhaps even more accurate would be the phrase 'a cut above something'. When we find a garment or another piece of merchandise that is outstanding, that has superior excellence, we use the expression that it is 'a cut above the rest'.[1]

This means that our God, who is uniquely holy, has no rivals or competition. He is transcendently separate from all others—above and beyond His little creatures.

'Holiness' is a word that is frequently used in the Old Testament of inanimate objects: in this sense it means that they were 'separated', set apart, or 'consecrated', to God for use in some aspect of His service or worship. Clearly, such things could not make choices, nor did they have a moral dimension or character to them: they were simply set apart for God's service. We, however, are not inanimate things but have been made in the image and likeness of God. This image has been marred and damaged by sin, but it has not been destroyed. When God brings someone to new birth, it is the beginning of the work of the full restoration of that image—a restoration that will ultimately conform us to the image of His dear Son—and we may say that the work of sanctification, of making us holy, has thus begun.

In one sense, we are immediately 'sanctified', in the sense that we are then 'set apart' for the Lord and His service. This appears to be the clear teaching of 1 Corinthians 6:11: 'you were washed, you were sanctified, you were justified in the name of the Lord Jesus Christ and by the Spirit of our God.' This is what the late Professor John Murray called 'definitive sanctification', because it has already occurred and it involves a decisive break with our past lives.[2] As Paul puts it in Romans 6:1–10, we have died to sin. Sin is, however, still very much active within us, and we now have to work out on a day-by-day basis the reality of living as those who have been set apart for the Lord and His service. Thus Paul can write to the Thessalonians, 'It is God's will that you should be sanctified' (1 Thessalonians 4:3). In 1 Corinthians 6:11 we learn that we *have been* sanctified; in 1 Thessalonians 4:3 we are told that God's will for us is that we *should be* sanctified. Clearly, although these two realities are closely related, they must be referring to different aspects of our sanctification. What is unmistakably clear from the surrounding context of both 1 Corinthians 6:11 and 1 Thessalonians 4:3 is that holiness is to have a clear *moral* dimension to it in our lives and characters.

Although God is altogether 'other' and different from

everything and everyone in the whole of creation, the Scriptures emphasize that *His* holiness is what makes our sanctification all the more necessary and compelling. Thus, one very helpful little booklet on this subject, by Hugh Morgan, is entitled *Holy God, Holy People*. The holiness of God is one of the reasons given in Scripture why we are commanded to live holy lives, lives which are different from those of the people around us: 'As obedient children, do not conform to the evil desires you had when you lived in ignorance. But just as he who called you is holy, so be holy in all you do' (1 Peter 1:14–15).

## BLIGHT OR BLESSING?

Our God is not only holy; He is awe-inspiring light (1 John 1:5). We need to be *in* that light and reflecting the glory of that light. To walk in the light brings glory to God. When we do not do so, we are walking in the shadows, or even in the dark. Our lifestyles must not be divorced from our professions of faith: confession of faith in Christ must be expressed in our conduct for Christ and that which is Christlike. God cannot use dirty 'tools'. Spurgeon underlines how essential a 'holy walk' is: 'God will not go to work with instruments which would compromise His own character . . . I beg you to attach the highest importance to your own personal holiness.'[3] God may choose not to use us: He is not beholden to us, nor, in the strictest sense of the word, does He *need* us (Acts 17:25).

We may say we believe certain things, but do our actions belie the things we say? We cannot have 'the talk without the walk'; we may delude ourselves—and sometimes others—

but we cannot fool God. Kevin de Young paraphrases some of Horatius Bonar's reflections on this subject:

Bonar . . . reminds us, holiness is not measured by 'one great heroic act or mighty martyrdom . . . It is of small things that a great life is made up.' Holiness is the sum of a million little things—the avoidance of little evils and little foibles, the setting aside of little bits of worldliness and little acts of compromise, the putting to death of little inconsistencies and little indiscretions, the attention to little duties and little dealings, the hard work of little self-denials and little self-restraints, the cultivation of little benevolences and little forbearances. Are you trustworthy? Are you kind? Are you patient? Are you joyful? Do you love? These qualities, worked out in all the little things of life, determine whether you are a blight or blessing to everyone around you.[4]

If we are careless about the way we live, and our lives are contrary to what God expects them to be, we will ultimately, and irrevocably, destroy ourselves. Here's a quote from Bonar himself:

If you are Christians then, be consistent. Be Christians out and out; Christians every hour, in every part, and in every matter. Beware of half-hearted discipleship, of compromise with evil, of conformity to the world, of trying to serve two masters—to walk in two ways, the narrow and the broad, at once. It will not do. Half-hearted Christianity will only dishonour God, while it makes you miserable.[5]

### ONE MIND WITH GOD

What, then, is true Christian practical holiness? How can we promote such holiness in our lives? J. C. Ryle explains, 'Holiness is the habit of being of one mind with God . . . hating what He hates, loving what He loves . . . He who most entirely agrees with God, he is the most holy . . . person.'[6]

We are to think God's thoughts, delighting in those things that delight Him, avoiding those things that pain Him, and embracing and executing God's commands as though He were speaking directly to us and expecting our unwavering obedience to His instructions. This is holiness. But of course, it does not come automatically. It is a lifelong process. The oldest saints on earth will still, even on their deathbeds, need to wrestle with the remnants of sin. We will grapple with our corruption until our last breath is taken. Death is the very last enemy with which we will have to contend. Until that time we need to fight on and 'watch [our] life and doctrine closely' (1 Timothy 4:16).

We need much wisdom to live life in this fallen world. Wisdom, therefore, is something for which we should be praying every single day of our lives. The late Hugh Morgan expressed the importance of the holiness of God's people before 'a watching world':

When the unbeliever not only hears the powerful preaching of the gospel, but sees that gospel at work in the lives of men and women in holiness, then he is forced to acknowledge that the gospel is the power of God unto salvation, and must be given sincere and serious consideration. The preacher should be able to point to his congregation and say, 'Here they are. Look at them, trophies of grace, and that grace in evidence in their daily lives.' . . . A holy life is the most efficient way of reducing the 'credibility gap' in the life of the church, that is the gap between life and behaviour . . . The preaching of the gospel is made considerably harder when there is want of consistent holy living in the flock.[7]

Holiness, when viewed and taken seriously, means all-out war on sin. In 1 Thessalonians 4:1 Paul says he has instructed the Christians on how to live 'in order to please God . . . more and more': we bring pleasure to Him in seeking to be like our Saviour, in living lives that are different from the lifestyles of the world around us. We are to fly in the face of current trends that lead us away from God's blueprint for life. J. C. Ryle expressed matters simply and succinctly when he wrote of the damage which can be wrought by a compromised life: 'I believe there is far more harm done by unholy and inconsistent Christians than we are aware of. Such men are among Satan's best allies. They pull down by their lives what ministers build with their lips . . . They supply the children of this world with a never-ending excuse for remaining as they are.'[8]

## STAY IN THE CENTRE

We are no longer to '[gratify] the cravings of our flesh . . . following its desires and thoughts' (Ephesians 2:3). We are to be separate, not deviating to the right or to the left, but staying in the centre of that 'highway of holiness'.

The story is told of an aristocratic lady in an earlier century who needed a driver for her horse-drawn coach. Three men applied for the position. They were asked a simple question that each in turn answered: 'If you were driving along a narrow road which had a very steep precipice at the side, how close to the edge would you be able to drive and still keep the carriage safely on the road?' The first man boasted that he would be able to drive within a yard (about a metre) of the edge and still be able to keep the carriage safely on the road. The second bragged that he would be able to go much closer to the edge: he could drive safely a foot (about a third of a metre) from where the road fell sharply away. The third man's response was very different and very definite— and it procured him the job: 'Oh, I wouldn't try such an experiment! I always keep as far from danger as is possible.' Do we experiment with how near we can live to the 'edge' of the world? If we do, we travel alone: holiness cannot walk that way! May we keep in step with the Spirit of God, walking on His highway. God the Holy Spirit has been given to help us in our endeavours after godliness: He is with us. We are not bereft; we have the Spirit of truth who will lead us into *all* truth and who will aid us in our every step. Gottfried Osei-Mensah comments upon this wonderful holy Friend:

He is not the comfort we get when we trust in Christ; He is the Comforter . . . If you received a package of explosives, you would have to decide what to do with it. But if you were favored with the visit of a dignitary, he more or less decides what to do with you! You are at His disposal. The Lord Jesus promises His people not 'parcels of power' but the powerful person of the Holy Spirit to stay with them.[9]

Jesus said, 'Remain in me, as I also remain in you. No branch can bear fruit by itself; it must remain in the vine' (John 15:4). Tom Wright defines the close relationship that Christ has with His people, even when He is pruning away the dead branches: 'Though it always hurts, we must be ready for the father's knife. God is glorified, and so will we be, by bearing good quality fruit, and lots of it . . . The vine-dresser is never closer to the vine, taking more thought over its long-term health and productivity, than when he has the knife in his hand.'[10]

## NO GRUBBY LIFESTYLE

While it is essential that we seek to cultivate the fruit of the Spirit in the way we live, we are never to forget that it is only through the work of the Spirit of God that we are able to achieve anything or do that which pleases Him. It is the blessed Spirit who shows us Christ in all His beauty and promotes Him. As F. Dale Brunner has said, 'The Holy Spirit does not mind being Cinderella outside the ballroom, if the Prince is honored inside His kingdom!'[11] It is He alone who gives us the desire to be like our Saviour. Being holy Himself, the Spirit wants to promote our holiness. He is like the floodlights which light up a cathedral: one does not see the floodlights, but one does see the cathedral in all its magnificent splendour. 'This perfectly illustrates the Spirit's new covenant role. He is, so to speak, the hidden floodlight shining on the Saviour. The Holy Spirit points us to Christ.'[12]

As one of the Puritans put it, 'The Sun is at its hottest when it is at its highest.' Our Lord Jesus has gone up on high, for the highest place that heaven affords is His by Sovereign right, and from heaven He pours out His Spirit into our hearts. This means He is nearer to us now than He was to the disciples when He walked the earth, for He dwells in us by His Spirit.[13]

With such a welcome guest we cannot have a 'grubby' lifestyle. Therefore, a major part of our endeavour to be holy must be *dealing with known sin in our lives*. We need to keep short accounts with God, and never allow particles of sin to amass between ourselves and Him or between us and others. The closer we walk with God and the more we familiarize ourselves with how He wants us to live, the more sensitive we will be to the way we speak, act and think. Is what I say or do in accordance with the character and will of God? Am I portraying the family likeness? Would the Lord Jesus be happy with the way I spoke to that person? Is my blessed Saviour being promoted in my every action? Am I a good reflection of Him? Some may never read the Bible but they will 'read' our lives.

### SLAY THE MONSTER

The pursuit of holiness also means that we are to *follow the path of self-denial*. 'Me-ism' is one of the biggest monsters we have to slay, especially at the present time. We can observe 'me-ism' all around us, as well as within ourselves. My husband and I took a summer holiday during the period when I was writing this book. During that holiday I lost count of the times when I saw parents concentrating on their phones or tablets, or simply intent on getting a good tan, all the while being utterly oblivious to their children's needs. Selfishness breeds selfishness. 'From all such selfishness, good Lord, deliver us, we pray.'

It goes without saying that if I am to prefer the needs or interests of someone else, I have to fade into the background. It would be ludicrous if the MC whose job it was to introduce musicians at a concert were to spend only a fraction of the time on this and filled the remainder of the evening giving information about himself, his work, his leisure time and the hobbies he enjoyed pursuing. We would rightly say that he had forgotten why he was there. But this can be precisely the problem with ourselves: we who are saved can forget our 'script'. Why are we here? Why have we been saved from 'death, destruction and despair'?[14] Do we forget that we are to honour Jesus Christ and please Him? One of the things that pleases Him is for us to become like Him in preferring the needs and interests of others to our own. Is this not what those magnificent words in Philippians 2:1–13 are all about?

We cannot 'promote' both ourselves and Jesus Christ. Since it is the purpose of God that in all things Jesus Christ should be pre-eminent (Colossians 1:18), we truly fulfil the purpose for which we were created when we seek to put Christ first in all things. When we do this, we gain a proper view of other people—of their needs and interests. It is the world that cries, 'Give me, give me, give me.' The world is only concerned with its own needs and wishes. It should not be so with those who desire holiness. Our response to the cross should be that of denying self and serving others. 'Whoever wants to be my disciple must deny themselves and take up their cross and follow me' (Matthew 16:24). We are to be characterized by love and good works—constantly giving ourselves to those around us. The Word of God should be our companion as we tread this road. If we fail to read the Bible and meditate on it, we will become like Samson shorn of his hair: our strength will be gone.

### LOVING RESPECT

In our pursuit we are to *fear God*. As we have seen already, this does not mean that we have a craven, cringing fear that torments us and engenders bondage; rather, it is a loving respect, a fear of offending Him and of disobeying Him, remembering that He sees all we do, say and think, even to the very depths of our subconscious. We should be concerned never to bring disgrace upon His Name. This is the way of holiness and a closer walk with God. Packer reminds us that

God's love is stern, for it expresses holiness in the lover and seeks holiness for the beloved. Scripture does not allow us to suppose that because God is love we may look at Him to confer happiness on people who will not seek holiness, or to shield His loved ones from trouble when He knows that they need trouble to further their sanctification.[15]

The story is told of a young boy who was urged by some companions to get involved in something that was utterly shameful. When he refused to do so, one of the gang mocked him, saying that he was afraid of what his father would do to him. The boy replied, 'No, I am afraid of what it would do to my father.' That showed a true reverence for his father, and the fear of God is like that. Of course, because God is infinitely greater than we are, the fear of God also means that we will be conscious of the fact that if we do displease Him, He may well chasten us for our sin: 'Consider therefore the kindness and sternness of God' (Romans 11:22).

### FLAT TYRES?

There are no short cuts to walking closely with God. There can be no pretending. Our lack of seeking to be holy, dealing with known sin in our lives and practising self-denial soon becomes apparent not just to ourselves, but to others as well. Maurice Roberts expresses it thus:

To keep the power of godliness in the soul is about the most difficult thing the Christian can do. A violin hung up on the wall soon goes out of tune . . . So does the soul, because of indwelling sin, soon lose its spiritual 'edge' . . . and become un-tuned for communion with God and other spiritual exercises . . . We betray the neglect of communion with God in private. The vehicle of devotion still travels along, but it is obvious that the tyres are flat and the whole machine is in need of an overhaul.[16]

## STAY ON THE PATH

It is through the Scriptures, both read and meditated upon in private, and heard read and preached publicly, that God will begin to shape and fashion us into His likeness. These exercises do not *make* us mature, but God uses such spiritual disciplines to help us grow. We are to sit daily at the feet of Jesus.[17] Sadly, often it is not Christ to whom we listen, but ourselves, or other Christians, the devil or the world. We may think that there is an easier way, or may even assure ourselves that a little compromise will do no harm, but that really is not true. If we look at Christian in *The Pilgrim's Progress*[18] we discover how he fared thinking such thoughts. Many were the trials that befell him on the way to the Celestial City, some the result of him looking for a more agreeable way to heaven. One of his first trials came when he met Formality and Hypocrisy, but he withstood the test they presented to him, and with great resolve climbed the Hill Difficulty, while Formality turned into a great forest called Danger, and

Hypocrisy went down the road of Destruction. As he climbed the hill Christian sang,

I must climb up to the mountain top;
Never mind if the path is steep,
For I know that through strife lies the way to life,
And the way-farer must not weep.
So courage! my heart, don't faint, don't fear,
Though the rough rock makes the way slow,
The easy track only leads me back,
Up and on is the way I must go![19]

However, a little further along on his journey Christian found the going very hard and he was not quite so determined. He soon discovered an easier road through By-path Meadow, and as a result found himself in the grip of Giant Despair! It was through the use of the key of faith that he escaped and, in spite of 'many dangers, toils and snares',[20] he *did* persevere to the end and reach his destination, the Celestial City. We may well ask: will we? To do so we must keep our eyes firmly fixed on the goal. We may fall while on the 'good ship Salvation', but the Lord's true people will not fall off that vessel: with faith, determination and God's unfailing help, we too will make it to our journey's end.

It is with such resolve that we are, as Martin Luther put it in his hymn, to 'fight the good fight', and 'Whatever [our] hand finds to do, do it with all [our] might' (Eccles. 9:10a). We are to work at being the best wife, mother, daughter, friend or helper we can be. And that should be our attitude in any other role or job in which we are employed. A sure way to please God is to follow God's way in the direction of 'home'. We cannot hope to attain a Christlike resemblance unless we stay on the path and follow in Christ's footsteps.

To him who is able to keep you from stumbling and to present you before his glorious presence without fault and with great joy—to the only God our Saviour be glory, majesty, power and authority, through Jesus Christ our Lord, before all ages, now and for evermore! (Jude 24–25)

## Food for thought

1. *Do your actions belie your profession? If so, explore the reasons why that could be.*
2. *How can you please God 'more and more'?*
3. *Are you in danger of 'driving your carriage' too close to the precipice?*
4. *How can you become more sensitive to your sin?*
5. *How can you become less self-indulgent?*
6. *As a Christian, what should be your attitude in everything you do?*

### Notes

1 Sproul, *Holiness of God*, p. 40.

2 Murray, *Collected Writings*, p. 277.

3 Spurgeon, *Soul Winner* (2001), p. 12.

4 De Young, *Hole in Our Holiness*, p. 145.

5 Horatius Bonar, *Light and Truth*, Volume 3: *The Acts and Larger Epistles* (London: James Nisbet & Co., 1869), p. 305; online at https://archive.org/stream/HoratiusBonarHoratiusBonar/Horatius%20Bonar%20-%20Light%20%26%20Truth%20Acts%20and%20Larger%20Epistles_djvu.txt.

6 Ryle, *Holiness*, p. 34.

**7** Morgan, *Holy God, Holy People*, pp. 56–57.

**8** Ryle, *Holiness*, p. 41.

**9** Quoted in Beeke and Thomas, *Holy Spirit and Reformed Spirituality*, p. 259.

**10** Wright on John 15:1–8, *John for Everyone*, p. 71.

**11** Quoted in Beeke and Thomas, *Holy Spirit and Reformed Spirituality*, p. 92.

**12** Packer, *Keep in Step with the Spirit*, p. 66.

**13** Beeke and Thomas, *Holy Spirit and Reformed Spirituality*, p. 89, quoting David Jones, *A Gracious, Willing Guest: The Indwelling Holy Spirit*.

**14** From William Gadsby's hymn 'Immortal Honours Rest on Jesus' Head'.

**15** Packer, *Knowing God*, p. 135.

**16** Roberts, *Great God of Wonders*, p. 5.

**17** See Appendix 6, 'Sitting at Jesus' Feet'.

**18** Bunyan, *Pilgrim's Progress*, p. 41.

**19** Ibid., p. 44.

**20** From John Newton's hymn 'Amazing Grace'.

# 8 Not automatic: growing in grace

*Grow in . . . grace . . . (2 Peter 3:18a)*

*. . . grace and truth came through Jesus Christ. (John 1:17b)*

*God's children improve all advantages to advance their grand
end; they labour to grow better by blessings and crosses,
and to make sanctified use of all things. (Richard Sibbes)*

As Christians we live in the realm of grace: our
lives began with grace and they will end with
grace. Without grace nobody can be a Christian,
however well they may think they live. Nothing
we have looked at thus far can be known without God's
amazing grace. Timothy Lane and Paul David Tripp declare,
'We are to celebrate a grace that not only forgives, but
changes us from the deepest, darkest corners of our hearts
to the smallest action and every idle word.'[1] And that should
be the compass of our change! We should not be excusing
or justifying actions and words that fall way below the
profession we make.

When I first became a Christian I remember the joy I felt at
being part of the family of God and at the real privilege of my
union with Christ and other believers. But the love and delight
I had at being part of God's family clouded my judgement.
I found myself defending a fellow Christian with whom my
unbelieving mother worked, even though this true sister in
the Lord was given to constant gossip. I discovered later that

there were just grounds for the criticisms which her work colleagues—my mother included—made of her. It was only by sharing the situation with another Christian that I realized that I had been wrong in seeking to defend the indefensible. Through wishing to defend a fellow believer I was, in effect, excusing her shoddy behaviour before those who rightly expected better things of her as a Christian. I was able, in measure, to right the situation: I confessed my error and directed my mother to the Saviour of sinners, encouraging her to gaze on Him and not on others. I suggested that she should not take her cue from those whom God was still refining. I also asked the Lord to give to me and to my 'sister in the faith' all the grace we needed not to fall below our privileges and muddy the reflection of Christ in us before others. We need God's grace moment by moment, and He willingly gives us all we need throughout each and every day.

**ONLY A PHONE CALL AWAY**

A Christian builder I know was once involved in a substantial building contract for a Christian organization some distance from where his business was located. He also had a number of other contracts on which he was working at the same time. This meant that he had to move from job to job in order to ensure that each contract was being properly fulfilled and was progressing according to plan. One day he was visiting the site where work for the Christian organization was being carried out. Before leaving to move on to the next site, he was overheard to say to his men, 'Remember, if there is anything— and I mean anything—that you need for the job, all you have to do is phone the office and we shall get it sent down. It's only a phone call away.' What an illustration of our position as Christians! God has a great building project in progress: 'In him the whole building is joined together and rises to become a holy temple in the Lord. And in him you too are being built together to become a dwelling in which God lives by his Spirit' (Ephesians 2:21–22). We are involved in this astounding kingdom work, and our gracious God can be contacted at any time, night or day, and can supply every resource imaginable for the job! 'Now to him who is able to do immeasurably more than all we ask or imagine . . .' (Ephesians 3:20). It's grace, grace and more grace, ever abounding, like a mighty waterfall cascading right to where we stand.

### GIVEN, GRASPED OR SQUANDERED?

As well as receiving grace for our *work*, Christ's grace should define, motivate and put into perspective our *giving*:[2] 'For you know the grace of our Lord Jesus Christ, that though he was rich, yet for your sake he became poor, so that you through his poverty might become rich' (2 Corinthians 8:9). Our riches in Christ are beyond all earthly riches, but He still gives us our 'daily bread', in addition to the wealth of spiritual blessings we receive through Him. He gives us everything we need. What a bountiful God is ours! He owns everything we are and have. We are, as Randy Alcorn says, just 'the managers of the assets God has entrusted . . . to us'.[3] 'Our giving is a reflexive response to the grace of God in our lives . . . It comes from the transforming work of Christ in us . . . This grace is the action; our giving is the reaction.'[4]

God gives what He owns; we are simply to regard ourselves as His stewards. But we can so easily abuse what God lends us, holding on to these things as if we had exclusive rights over them, with little regard for others. There is a grace in giving. 'God loves a cheerful giver' (2 Corinthians 9:7b). John Piper comments, 'I take this to mean that God is not pleased when people act benevolently but don't do it gladly. When people don't find pleasure (Paul's word is cheer) in their acts of service, God doesn't find pleasure in them. He loves cheerful givers, cheerful servants.'[5]

We are to remember that though our work is done *below*, we will have to give an account *above* of all we have given, grasped or squandered. Romans 14:10, 12 states that 'we will all stand before God's judgment seat . . . each of us will give an account of ourselves to God'.

The Macedonian church is able to teach us not just about giving, but about *cheerful, generous giving*. When they gave to help the hungry Christians in Jerusalem, it was an act of grace on their part: their giving came not out of a full bank account, but out of extreme poverty; and it was given not just joyfully, but from 'overflowing joy and . . . rich generosity' (2 Corinthians 8:2). Even when deterred by others who were aware of their poverty, the grace of giving that had welled up within them could not be quelled. Rather, Paul writes, 'they urgently pleaded with us for the privilege of sharing in this service to the Lord's people' (8:4).

What challenging words! Do we regard our giving as a privilege? Do we give joyfully and sacrificially? What counts is not so much the amount we give, but how much we have left over in proportion to what we give, and the attitude of our giving. If we remember that all we possess is God's, we will not be afraid to put back into His hands what He has given us

**HIS TREASURED POSSESSION**

on loan. Jesus said, 'Give, and it will be given to you. A good measure, pressed down, shaken together and running over, will be poured into your lap. For with the measure you use, it will be measured to you' (Luke 6:38). This means that the standard of 'generosity' we adopt will be used likewise for us.

God gives us well in excess of what we deserve, so what a magnanimous response should be ours! In answer to the question 'Why has He provided [us] with so much?', Alcorn writes,

God comes right out and tells us why He gives us more money than we need. It's not so we can find ways to spend it. It's not so we can indulge ourselves and spoil our children. It's not so we can insulate ourselves from needing God's provision. It's so we can give—generously. When God provides more money, we often think, 'This is a blessing.' Well, yes, but it would be just as scriptural to think, 'This is a test.'[6]

In 2 Corinthians 9:10–11 Paul gives the scriptural warrant for Alcorn's assessment. He states quite plainly that our giving has consequences: when we are tight-fisted, we fail to *know* joy in giving, and we also fail to *bring* joy to God. God will not see His image in us if we are mean and miserly. As we give, God loves to give to us, although that should not be the motivation for our giving. 'God's shovel is so much bigger than ours,' said R. G. LeTourneau.[7]

### ARE WE COASTING?

It is by God's grace, and His grace alone, that we are able to be built up in a holy faith and to grow in grace; our giving should be a natural overflow of the grace found in our lives. To grow in grace is to learn to appreciate the never-ending grace of

God in us. It is through the indwelling of the Holy Spirit that the Christian life is to be lived—in utter dependence upon Him. I again quote Lane and Tripp:

It is so easy to coast! We have been accepted into God's family and some day will be with Him in eternity. But what goes on in between? From the time we came to Christ to the time we go to be with Him, God calls us to change. We have been changed by His grace, are being changed by His grace, and will be changed by His grace.[8]

We need to scrutinize ourselves: every idle thought, attitude and motive. Have our lives been changed? Are they being changed? Do we desire an ongoing change? We need daily to confess our sin (we will deal with confession in Part 2). As well as this daily acknowledgement of our sin, there are certain seasons when we need to give particular thought to our transgressions: it may be before the Lord's Day, or Communion. Are we aware of any known sin in our lives that we need to confess, and which is especially stunting our growth? Or again, we may have an important date in the calendar—for example, our birthday. Some go to extravagant lengths to celebrate this day in their lives. If we do nothing else on our birthday, what a splendid opportunity it is to give thanks to God for all His loving-kindness, support and sustaining grace through another year, and to search our hearts before Him. Robert Murray M'Cheyne used each birthday as an opportunity to gauge his spiritual progress from one year to the next. We are not as practised as our forefathers were in such exercises, and we can be poor judges of our own condition, but those who know us best, and love us most, could help and exhort us in this area. But it needs to be constantly stressed that this growth is not automatic. We grow or we decline, and our choice affects not only ourselves, but also our nearest and dearest, the fellow Christians in our churches and, above all, God and His glory. Thomas Watson describes the outcome of our failure to grow: 'The lowest degree of grace will bring salvation to you, but not much glory to God.'[9]

## IS GOD OUTSIDE THE DOOR?

As the Westminster Confession declares, our chief end, above lesser ones, is 'to glorify God and to enjoy Him for ever'. If we do not glorify and enjoy Him now, we will find when we reach glory that much of our lives was redundant—or we may even have the pain of discovering that we built on the wrong foundation, with the wrong building tools, and our lives may come crashing down around us (Matthew 7:24–27). We may discover too late that heaven was not our home after all. One of the problems of the 'Babel building' was that unity between the builders was higher on their agenda than unity with God and enjoying His presence. He had been pushed right out of their reckoning, so God had to 'visit' them (see Genesis 11:5): they thought only of their own glory. Sadly, this can be our problem today: we can have great enjoyment in being together; we can be taken up with our projects; but we have left God outside the door.

If our whole lives are built on Christ, and our focus is on growing in grace in order to glorify God, then we can be assured of His undivided attention in helping us to mature as Christians. As we progress, step by step, in exercising love, developing faith, adding to our knowledge, promoting holiness and growing in grace, the more the image of our Saviour will be stamped upon our souls, and this will find expression in the way we live. John Owen describes the believer who is journeying nearer 'home': 'As rivers, the nearer they come to the ocean whither they tend, the more they increase their waters, and speed their streams; so will grace flow more fully and freely in its near approaches to the ocean of glory.'[10]

Are we looking for that home-going? Not one of us knows when that day will dawn and we will be called to 'higher service'.

The Word became flesh and made his dwelling among us. We have seen his glory, the glory of the one and only Son, who came from the Father, full of grace and truth. (John 1:14)

## Food for thought

1. *What areas of our lives is grace meant to touch and change?*

2. *Where should we, as Christians, look for the resources to love?*

3. *How is progression in our lives as Christians manifested?*

4. *What should we do if, upon examination, we become conscious that we are 'coasting'?*

### Notes

**1**  Lane and Tripp, *Change Is Possible*, p. 16.

**2**  See Appendix 7, 'My Giving Covenant'.

3  See Appendix 8, 'Treasure Principle Keys'.

4  Alcorn, *Treasure Principle*, p. 31.

5  Piper, *Desiring God* (2011), p. 120.

6  Alcorn, *Treasure Principle*, pp. 74–75.

7  Quoted in ibid., pp. 73–74.

8  Lane and Tripp, *Change Is Possible*, p. 15.

9  Thomas Watson, *A Body of Practical Divinity* (1833), quoted in Roberts, *Great God of Wonders*, p. 36.

10 Owen, *Person of Christ*, p. 433.

**HIS TREASURED POSSESSION**

# 9 Weighing in

*Make every effort to add to your faith goodness . . .*
*knowledge . . . self-control . . . perseverance . . . godliness*
*. . . mutual affection . . . [and] love. For if you possess*
*these qualities in increasing measure, they will keep*
*you from being ineffective and unproductive in your*
*knowledge of our Lord Jesus Christ. (2 Peter 1:5–8)*

*Resolution One: I will live for God.*
*Resolution Two: If no one else does, I will. (Jonathan Edwards)*

How can we apply to our lives all that we have looked at in the previous chapters? We have viewed our goal and seen ways in which we can achieve it: by exercising ourselves to grow in love, faith, knowledge, holiness and grace. But what if we feel we are spiritually out of shape, and out of touch with God?

I remember, just after enrolling at the gym, seeing the beginning of a programme on television entitled *The Biggest Loser*. The programme had nothing to do with money, exams or prestige, but was about *weight*! The only part of the programme I watched was the weighing-in of the people taking part in the show. Most of them did not know just how overweight they were. They looked totally shocked when their actual weight in kilos flashed across the screen. Fortunately for us, we do not have our 'spiritual weight' written large for others to see; we can have a private consultation with God Himself. It is when we read the correct assessment of ourselves in the Bible, with conviction of the Holy Spirit upon our hearts and minds, that we begin to see just how out of shape we are, spiritually speaking.

Sadly, our lack of spiritual strength may be due to the fact that we are keeping more in tune with the world's way of thinking than with God's. We need to 'put off' the flab and 'put on' the muscle! Ephesians 4:17, 22–24 tells us, 'You must no longer live as the Gentiles do . . . You were taught . . . to put off your old self . . . ; to be made new in the attitude of your minds; and to put on the new self, created to be like God in true righteousness and holiness.'

## A FLABBY LIFE

If we are imitating those around us, we are following the world's agenda rather than God's. Instead, we are to be holy people of God, set apart for Him, as 1 Peter 1:14–15 tells us emphatically: 'As obedient children, do not conform to the evil desires you had when you lived in ignorance. But just as he who called you is holy, so be holy in all you do.'

We can be subtly drawn back into our former ways of life—a flabby life! Apparently, a frog in warm water will not detect the change in temperature if the heat is increased only very gradually. There will be no attempt on the frog's part to jump out, even though the temperature may eventually reach boiling point and the frog be boiled to death. The same can be true of us: the world can seep into our lives, be it ever so slowly, and we may not detect the effect it is having upon us. Samuel Rutherford has excellent advice: 'Build your nest upon no tree here; for you see God has sold the forest to death.'[1]

I remember a missionary who was on home assignment

visiting a minister he knew. As he spent time with his friend, he was surprised and alarmed at what the minister-friend was watching on television. Three years before, when the missionary was on home assignment, his friend would not have tolerated the things he now enjoyed. Sadly, such things had become part of his life, as they can so insidiously become part of ours. We have to stay close to God, not to this world, if we wish to be safe. Also, this is how we declare our love for Him. James 4:4a says, 'Don't you know that friendship with the world means enmity against God?'

### FALLING INTO THE DEVIL'S SNARE

The world can be writing our agenda, often shouting at us, 'You won't be happy until you have this, this and this!' Leisure and pleasure are screaming at us through a megaphone and being trumpeted from every conceivable place. Is our contentment based on *these things* or on God alone? We need to ask ourselves: Does my happiness depend on *things* and *plans*, or is it based on Christ? That is not to say that we are forbidden to enjoy the good things He has freely and bountifully given us in this world; rather, it is a matter of priorities. God's Word tells us, 'Godliness with contentment is great gain' (1 Timothy 6:6). We should not be endlessly striving for things we cannot or should not have. If we are discontented, we need to ask ourselves if this is the reason why. If we are no longer enjoying the things of God—or, more tellingly, God Himself—we need to ask ourselves the reason for this.

I remember, when my husband was first in the ministry, having a day out with him in a large city. I had so looked forward to the day because at that time we lived in a somewhat out-of-the-way place. Having left the children with a friend, we really enjoyed the opportunity to have some valuable time alone together. However, as we were returning home I became aware of feeling rather down. Seeking to analyse the reason for my low spirits, I soon realized it was because I could not have the things I had seen and desired. It was then I recognized that I had fallen into the devil's snare: the Lord Christ *and* things, not 'Christ alone'.[2]

So easy to desire what others have,
Instead of seeing all the gifts that you have given me.
So help me fan the flame which you began,
And burn in me a love for you that all will clearly see.[3]

We need to take heed and beware of coveting what others have and, perhaps, we cannot own. Covetousness is idolatry! I had to confess to being an idolater that day. When our trust shifts from God to things, we can slowly fall into the realm of idolatry—*it can creep up on us!* It can also strip us of the fruit that God is trying to cultivate in our lives. Our contentment in God and all that He so freely gives us in a multitude of ways can take wings and fly away, leaving us as spiritual paupers. The very root of our growth and enjoyment, which is God Himself, is cut off. Richard Bernard, a Puritan pastor and prolific writer, wrote, 'A godly man prefers grace before goods, and wisdom before the world.'[4] The devil is waiting in the wings, watching for the moment when we take our eyes off our Saviour and transfer them to 'things'.

Riches I heed not, nor man's empty praise:
Be thou mine inheritance, now and always;

Be thou and thou only the first in my heart;
O high King of heaven, my *treasure* thou art.[5]

We can never afford to take time out from 'training'.

## THE DEVIL'S GOALS FOR US

But if it only meant that we sought to be content, that we applied rigorous discipline and exercise to our lives, that we pursued God and His work diligently—then in no time at all many (if not all) of us would be monuments to His grace and a tremendous witness to the world. But we are not in heaven yet, and life is not quite so simple and straightforward, because every desire we have for our own souls and for others will be opposed by the devil. We have considerable forces arrayed against us: we have our sin to contend with, the devil to wrestle against and a world that seeks to weaken our endeavours. So the fight is on, every single day that the Lord is pleased to keep us on this earth.

The devil is working furiously against us. And we forget this warfare at our peril. What are *the devil's goals* for us? First and foremost, he wants to use us like pawns to bring disgrace on Jesus Christ. The Father wants to bring His Son honour and glory; the devil wants to destroy God's purpose. If the devil can use the very people who have been redeemed to pour contempt on Christ through the way they live, great will be his triumph. Satan wants us to fail in our 'chief end', which is to live godly lives and enjoy living them to God's glory. He wants us to be distracted by the world, so we do not have time to give to God and to get to know Him better. And he is determined to make us ineffective in our witness to a needy world. When he has done all this, he has won a resounding victory. He has succeeded in making us weak, ineffectual Christians, not fit for the work for which Christ has called us. K. F. Prior reminds us of our calling:

Satan is a malignant reality, always hostile to God and to God's people. But he has already been defeated in Christ's life and death and resurrection, and this defeat will become obvious and complete in the end of the age . . . God needs his people as witnesses. It is here, right in the midst of evil, that a Christian is called upon to exhibit the power of grace, to show forth his faith, courage and patience as a good soldier of Jesus Christ.[6]

Something which can help us in this fight is constantly reminding ourselves that there is a battle in the heavenly places against all God's people: it is not a solo contest (1 Peter 5:9). Christ is praying that our faith will not fail, while the devil is urging us to concede to his wishes so that we fall short of our goal. Each time we fail the Lord we should be aware that somewhere along the line the devil has had a hand in it and is exultant. That very thought should spur us on all the more to want to please Christ, to obey His commands and to live lives that will bring Him credit, not shame. Our objective should be to bring glory to His wonderful Name. We were redeemed at such a cost (1 Peter 1:19)! 'The Lord Jesus Christ . . . gave himself for our sins to rescue us from the present evil age' (Galatians 1:3b–4a).

### SLIPPING, STATIC OR STANDING?
If we are feeling dry and jaded, having experienced the onslaughts of the enemy or having wandered from 'the shelter of the Most High' (Psalm 91:1), we can go back to the Lord

and tell Him that we are out of shape, have stayed static or have even slipped back. We can ask for His help to love Him and others. God is willing to support and comfort us so that we may know and trust Him better. He will grant His Holy Spirit to shape our lives and help transform them.

If, however, we are going on steadily and contentedly, we *must not* fail to thank and praise Him for His keeping power. But we need to remember that there is always room for growth in love, faith and every other grace, so that we may bring delight to our Saviour. If we bear His Name, we must also bear His character! John Stott puts succinctly many of the points I have been making:

I venture to urge you to be patient, but determined. Do not lose heart. Watch the discipline of your Christian life. Be diligent in daily prayer and Bible reading, in church-going and attendance at the Lord's Supper. Make good use of your Sundays. Read helpful books. Seek out Christian friends. Get busy in some form of service. Never leave your sins un-confessed and un-forgiven. Never allow a pocket of resistance to arise in your heart. Above all, yield yourself without reserve each day to the power of the Holy Spirit who is within you. Then step by step you will advance along the road of holiness, and grow towards full spiritual maturity.[7]

## Food for thought

1. *How can we determine our 'spiritual weight' and assess our fitness?*
2. *Whose agenda are you following?*
3. *Are you being 'boiled alive'? Have your Christian standards slipped as you have grown older as a Christian? Are you conforming to this world or to God's kingdom?*

*4. How can you demonstrate that you love God?*

*5. Is your contentment in God alone?*

**Notes**

1 Quoted in Gilbert, *Dictionary*, p. 206.

2 Stuart Townend and Keith Getty, 'In Christ Alone'.

3 Lou Fellingham, 'Build This House'.

4 'Puritan Quotes', https://www.gracegems.org/30/puritan_quotes.htm.

5 Mary Elizabeth Byrne (trans.), 'Be Thou My Vision'; emphasis added.

6 Prior, *Great Doctrines of the Bible*, pp. 107, 109.

7 Stott, *Christian Basics*, p. 44.

# Part 2. Value for knowing Him

# 10 My desire: desiring God

*I consider everything a loss because of the surpassing worth
of knowing Christ Jesus my Lord. (Philippians 3:8)*

*Jesus, Jesus, all sufficient,*
*Beyond telling is Thy worth;*
*In Thy Name lie greater treasures*
*Than the richest found on earth.*
*Such abundance*
*Is my portion with my God. (William Williams)*

I n his *Soliloquies*, Augustine of Hippo has a dialogue
with Reason. Reason asks him what he desires to know.
I wonder what our answer would be if we were asked the
same question? Augustine's reply is: 'God and the soul,
that is what I desire to know.' Reason asks, 'Nothing more?'
Augustine's response is: 'Nothing whatever.'[1] Calvin almost
echoes Augustine when at the beginning of his *Institutes* he
states, 'Our wisdom . . . consists of almost entirely two parts:
the knowledge of God and of ourselves.'[2] To know God and
ourselves—even in part—enables us to get a foothold on life.

While writing this book, I had just started re-reading this
section when I took a coffee break. As I entered the refectory
of the university where I had been writing this book I saw a
woman I had got to know while using the library. She seemed
to live at her desk, not just on weekdays but throughout
the weekend. This time, she seemed quite distressed. When
I enquired of her as to the cause of her anxiety, she replied

that she was grappling at that moment with the thought of 'our little lives', and the 'little deaths within death', as she put it. She had explained to me some time earlier that her mother was in the last stages of Alzheimer's, so she may very well have been preoccupied with the thought of her mother, as well as of her own mortality. When I asked her further about this, I discovered that what she was trying to say was that we do not really know ourselves, and we do not know the hereafter. What a bleak and empty world the unbeliever moves in! 'God and the soul'; 'the knowledge of God and of ourselves': what an expanse lies in these words, and what comfort can be ours in and through them!

Spurgeon expands upon these sentiments in one of his sermons as he replies to the worldly man who scoffs at a poor Christian who is content in his knowledge of God and himself. He explains what riches belong to believers:

'What, poor man, are you perfectly content?' 'Yes,' says he, 'it is my Father's will that I should live in poverty. I am perfectly content.' 'Well, but is there nothing else you wish for?' 'Nothing,' says he, 'I have the presence of God; I have delight in communion with Christ; "I know that there is laid up for me a crown of life that fadeth not away", and more I cannot want. I am perfectly content; my soul is at rest.'[3]

### MY DETERMINED PURPOSE

The Scriptures are full of such thoughts. In Jeremiah 9:23–24 we read,

This is what the LORD says:
'Let not the wise boast of their wisdom
    or the strong boast of their strength

**HIS TREASURED POSSESSION**

> or the rich boast of their riches,
> but let the one who boasts boast about this:
> that they have the understanding to know me.'

In 2 Peter 1:3 the apostle Peter declares, 'His divine power has given us everything we need for a godly life through our knowledge of him who called us.' And there are many other verses that could be cited. Suffice it to say that, with the weight of the Bible, the encouragement of the 'divines' and the support of great and godly men like Spurgeon, we have sufficient proof that knowing God is essential for our comfort here and in the life to come, whatever our earthly circumstances might be. In fact, the most important experience we could ever have is that of truly knowing God.

In Part 1 we saw that godliness was a God-likeness—seeking to be like our Saviour, as in our fervent pursuit we grow to bear His likeness. But we should make it our goal not just to know about Christ, in becoming living, walking reflections of Him, but to experience that vital fellowship with our Saviour which gives us a deeper and more assured trust in His dealings with our lives in their entirety.

In the following chapters we will explore the ways in which we develop this experiential knowledge of God. Paul's intense longing to know Christ is captured in the Amplified Version of the Bible: '(For my determined purpose is) that I may know Him (that I may progressively become more deeply and intimately acquainted with Him, perceiving and recognizing and understanding the wonders of His Person more strongly and more clearly)' (Philippians 3:10, Amplified Version, Classic Edition). Jerry Bridges says,

This is the heartbeat of the godly person. As he contemplates God in the awesomeness of His infinite majesty, power and holiness, and then as he dwells upon the riches of God's mercy and grace poured out at Calvary, his heart is captivated by this One who could love him so. He is satisfied with God alone, but he is never satisfied with his present experience of God. He always yearns for more.[4]

### DEPTHS YET TO BE PLUMBED

Do we know anything of this yearning and longing for God? Do we realize that there are depths we have not yet plumbed in our experience of Him? Our beginning in the Christian life can be compared to little children who are learning to count with beads; like them, we need to progress from that stage, rather than being stuck there. Sadly, however, some of us are still counting on our fingers! We can read or hear of people's experiences of God and be enthralled by them, but we stop there. As finite creatures we shall, of course, never know God fully in all His immensity and transcendence, but just a 'glimpse' of Him will place us where we should be: prostrate in the dust. In such a position we will appreciate what fallen creatures we are, and this will cause us to worship and desire our Saviour in all His wonder yet more and more.

Spurgeon poses the question: 'Is it not time we should begin to live nearer to God?' May we not only have head knowledge, but also a heart aflame with yearning to draw *nearer* to our great God. We need our whole being—mind and soul—to be stretched to embrace the possibility of knowing Him in this way, so that we too, like Augustine, can truly say that our desire is to know God, and nothing more. In the next chapter we will look at this desire to know God. May it be our longing too!

Your name and renown
  are the desire of our hearts. (Isaiah 26:8b)

## Food for thought

1. *What is* the *most important experience we could ever have in this life?*
2. *What is the difference between a head knowledge and an experiential knowledge of God?*
3. *Is this experiential knowledge of God foreign to you?*

### Notes

1  Quoted in Roberts, *Thought of God*, p. 32.

2  Calvin, *Institutes*, p. 37.

3  Charles H. Spurgeon, *The Complete Works of C. H. Spurgeon*, Volume 5: *Sermons 225–285* (electronic edn; [USA]: Delmarva Publications, 2013), [n.p.].

4  Bridges, *Practice of Godliness*, p. 29.

# 11 Walk and talk: contact

*You, God, are my God,*
*earnestly I seek you;*
*I thirst for you,*
*my whole being longs for you,*
*in a dry and parched land*
*where there is no water.*
*(Psalm 63:1)*

*Let us occupy ourselves entirely in knowing God. The more*
*we know Him, the more we will desire to know Him. As love*
*increases with knowledge, the more we know God, the more*
*we will truly love Him. We will learn to love Him equally in*
*times of distress or in times of great joy. (Brother Andrew)*

Do we know what it is to walk and talk with Jesus every day? Are we conscious of living for someone else rather than for ourselves? As we come to look at this whole subject of knowing God in our experience, we need to stress again that there is a great difference between *knowing about God* and actually *knowing God experientially.* J. I. Packer explains, 'Knowing God is more than knowing about him; it is a matter of dealing with him as he opens up to you, and being dealt with by him as he takes knowledge of you. Knowing about him is a necessary precondition of trusting him.'[1]

Imagine if someone were to say that they knew the Queen when they had only gleaned facts about her from a magazine!

They might know a lot *about* the Queen, but having never met her personally they could hardly claim to *know* her. On one occasion in London, while queuing for a train ticket, my husband was reading a book by Os Guinness. He had noticed the author's photograph on the book's dust jacket and, glancing around, saw that Os Guinness was actually standing right behind him! Although he had learned something about the man by reading his book, he got to know him far better in the brief conversation that followed.

You could think of it like this. My mother-in-law was a championship swimmer, having been trained by someone who had been taught by an Olympic coach. By contrast, my late father-in-law could not swim a stroke: he would sink like a stone to the bottom of a pool if he attempted it. But as a young man he had read a book about learning to swim: the book encouraged one to lie on a couch or settee and practise the arm and leg movements of various swimming styles, and this he did assiduously. Alas! It is one thing to move one's arms and legs while lying on a settee, but doing the same thing in water is a very different matter! And since he never ventured from the security of the settee to the challenge of the swimming pool, it is no surprise that he never learned to swim. Or one might compare it to reading the theory book for a driving test while sitting in an armchair with a driving wheel in our hands. We may go through all the motions but never have first-hand experience of being on the road. Unless we get out of that chair, into the car and join the flow of traffic, we will never know what it is really like to drive. We will never have the thrill of driving in open country.

**HIS TREASURED POSSESSION**

## CONTACT, NOT CONTRACT

'Taste and see that the LORD is good,' says Psalm 34:8. The same is true with our experience of God. It is not enough only to read the Bible and become familiar with the facts about God: we must know the Author for ourselves. Jerry Bridges speaks in the following way of the desire that is stirred within us when we seek after God: 'True godliness engages our affections and awakens within us a desire to enjoy God's presence and fellowship. It produces a longing for God Himself.'[2]

When I was a student I was very friendly with a postgraduate who became like a 'father in the faith' to me. He shared with me all the doctrines of grace we find in the Bible, but as time went on I realized that though he possessed a great deal of knowledge about God—far more than I would ever know— he seemed to have little experience of actually *knowing* Him. Sadly, the last I heard of him was that he was no longer meeting with God's people. It is vitally important that we do not mistake knowledge *about* God for *knowing* Him. Packer underlines this when he writes, 'The width of our knowledge of God is no gauge of the depth of our knowledge of Him.'[3]

So how can we know our God in a deeper and more personal way? To help us answer this, let us ask another question: How does one get to know *any other person* in a deeper and more experiential way? The first thing is that we must have *contact* with that person. You cannot have a meaningful relationship with someone if you don't spend any time together. Knowing someone is intensely *personal*.

My husband and I have close friends who live in Germany. They have told us that it is not uncommon there for a husband to be working in one part of the country and for his wife to be working hundreds of miles away. The result is that a significant number of married couples live apart from each other during the week and only spend weekends together. In situations like this it is difficult to see how a couple can expect to develop a meaningful relationship together or build a happy marriage. The relationship and the marriage are bound to suffer. But I have met some Christians who give the impression that their relationship with God can be framed like a contract: 'Once I have done everything I need to do, then I promise [myself, God or both] I will spend some time with God.' But such an agreement is one-sided and is seldom kept. Has that not been our experience at some point in our lives? We are about to read and pray when something we planned to do later comes into our heads, so we go and do it; when that is done, it leads on to something else; and before we know it we are more than halfway through the day. Then the children come in, or there's that bit of DIY that we have been promising to do for months, or the dog needs a walk—and it may often be only as we are falling into bed that we remember we never did actually get round to having our time with the Lord! The devil is a master at orchestrating our lives, bringing alternative employment across our paths, so that God is conveniently pushed aside. We need to be on our guard against the devil and his many schemes to alienate us from the Lord.

## STAY WARM

*Contact* is vitally important if we want to develop a close friendship with God, just as it is with any other friendship. How can we hope to get to know someone if we are not willing to spend time with that person? Our reading of the

Word is God talking to us so that we may know His thoughts; *He* condescends to share with us. Dare we miss such an opportunity? R. C. Sproul identifies one of the causes of the lack of Bible reading amongst professing Christians:

Here, then, is the real problem of our negligence. We fail in our duty to study God's Word not so much because it is difficult to understand, not so much because it is dull and boring, but because it is work. Our problem is not a lack of intelligence or a lack of passion. Our problem is that we are lazy.[4]

The danger is that, because we think nobody else can see our lack of contact with God, we imagine we can get away with the minimum and still survive as Christians. (Jesus, of course, drew attention to the fact that our heavenly Father, who sees us in secret, will reward us openly, Matthew 6:6. So, contrary to what we may fondly imagine, others *will* know whether we have spent time with God or not.) God is faithful: He never fails us; the fault is ours alone. Augustine said with respect to our relationship with the Lord: 'When people choose to withdraw from a fire, the fire continues to give warmth, but they grow cold. When people choose to withdraw far from light, the light continues to be bright in itself, but they are in darkness. This is also the case when people withdraw from God.'[5] How dull and uninviting are the bare bars of an electric fire! And without the coals burning brightly, we are not encouraged to sit round a fireplace on a cold, grey day. This need not be our spiritual experience: drawn into close contact with God, we not only experience the warmth of fellowship with Him, but we also become conductors of that heat to others. Some may then want what we have found—or rather, the One we have found. Our contact with God will become *all I desire to know*. We must stay warm! 'The person who spends time with God radiates His glory in a manner that is always warm and inviting, never cold and forbidding.'[6]

## OVERTURES OF LOVE

God has stipulated the way in which we are to meet Him. We are to remember that He will not be friends with us on *our* terms. He says, 'You will seek me and find me when you seek me with all your heart' (Jeremiah 29:13). So it is essential to have regular contact with God, both for our own benefit and for the benefit of others.

As we have seen, the most obvious and regular way in which we meet with the Lord is through His Word (God speaking to us) and through prayer (our speaking to Him). But the prerogative in this relationship always lies with God. Packer, commenting on Psalm 139, describes the wonder of it: 'Just as there are no bounds to his presence with me, so there are no limits to his knowledge of me. Just as I am never left alone, so I never go unnoticed . . . Living becomes an awesome business when you realise that you spend every moment of your life in the sight and company of an omniscient Creator.'[7]

God watches over us and cares for us. What a privilege we have to be His children! He is always there, but He loves to be sought by us. Our response to God's overtures of love must surely be that of the psalmist:

You, God, are my God,
   earnestly I seek you;
I thirst for you,

> my whole being longs for you . . .
> Because your love is better than life,
>   my lips will glorify you.
> I will praise you as long as I live. (Psalm 63:1, 3)

This should be our natural response to a God who is constantly there for us, who neither slumbers nor sleeps (Psalm 121:4) and who is bent on our protection and our good. He rarely reveals Himself to those of His people who show little, if any, desire for Him; but He will certainly be found by those who earnestly seek Him: 'Seek and you will find' (Matthew 7:7). The way to God is ever open and accessible to us. We can enter the very throne room of the King of kings, by virtue of the blood of Jesus Christ. We can come at any time of day or night, whether a summer season is warming our souls or the chill winds of winter are blasting our spirits. We can enter when we are full of joy and eager to do God's will; we can enter with the same boldness when our hearts are heavy and our steps are wooden. Our heavenly Father is ready to hear and answer the merest whisper of prayer[8] with the same readiness with which He will listen to the boldest pleading at the throne of grace. Our prayers are the breathings of our soul, friend to Friend: *we* sharing with Him, He sharing with us. What an encouragement to know that it is as we pray that we grow to know the Lord of Glory better! And it is not just through prayer, but through every means of grace: reading God's Word; praying; hearing God's Word preached; participating in the Lord's Supper; and in fellowship with the saints. In all the vicissitudes of life God makes Himself known through the private and the public

**HIS TREASURED POSSESSION**

means of grace. So it is a two-way relationship: there must be contact.

I am the vine; you are the branches. If you remain
in me and I in you, you will bear much fruit; apart
from me you can do nothing. (John 15:5)

## Food for thought

1. *Do you know the enjoyment of living every day with Jesus?*

2. *What is the depth as well as the width of your knowledge of God?*

3. *How can we get to know God in a deeper and more personal way?*

4. *What are the means of grace whereby we can nurture our relationship with the Lord?*

### Notes

1  Packer, *Knowing God*, p. 38.

2  Bridges, *Practice of Godliness*, p. 28.

3  Packer, *Knowing God*, p. 38.

4  Quoted in Whitney, *Spiritual Disciplines*, p. 32.

5  Quoted at Quoty, http://www.quoty.org/quote/742.

6  Bridges, *Practice of Godliness*, p. 30.

7  Packer, *Knowing God*, pp. 90–91.

8  Even a sigh which cannot find expression in the words of prayer is a prayer in itself, drawn from deep emotion, which God Himself interprets and answers. Note Romans 8:26: 'We do not know what we ought to pray for, but the Spirit himself intercedes for us through wordless groans.'

# 12 Real and sweet: communion

*... that they may be one as we are one—I in them
and you in me—so that they may be brought
to complete unity. (John 17:22b–23a)*

*The union of Christians to Christ, their common head; and, by
means of the influence they derive from him, one to another,
may be illustrated by the loadstone. It not only attracts the
particles of iron to itself, by the magnetic virtue; but by this
virtue, it unites them one among another. (Richard Cecil)*

As well as contact with God, we also need *communion* with Him. We have been united with Christ in His death and resurrection. The bond of our union with Him will never be severed. Whatever our mood, whether high or low, our union with Him remains stable and sure; but it may often be the case that because of our ups and downs, our ill-discipline or the storms of life, we drift or are blown off-course, and our communion with Christ is not always as real as it might be or as sweet as we would like. Maurice Roberts explains the difference between the terms 'union' and 'communion':

We make a distinction between our union with Christ and our communion with Him. The union is always there and cannot be broken. But the communion which we have with Christ in this life is our felt, conscious enjoyment of His love. This is by no means constant, but varies from day to day and from hour to hour. The mature believer's supreme desire is, as was George Whitefield's, to have the enjoyment of a 'felt Christ'.[1]

The communion Christ had with His Father was vital: daily, hourly, indeed moment by moment. He was never out of touch with the One whom He obeyed and for whom He lovingly worked. Christ had no sin that could alter His constant view and enjoyment of His Father. He prayed for this same intimacy of communion with His Father for all those who were His: '. . . that they may be one as we are one—I in them and you in me—so that they may be brought to complete unity' (John 17:22b–23a).

## ONE TOGETHER

The union with our Saviour which all believers share inevitably leads to a union which we have with each other: that is to say, the 'vertical union' with Christ entails a 'horizontal union' with all who belong to Him. In other words, it produces *community*: Christ and His Father are one, Christ and His people are one, and *all* Christ's people are one. Since our union with Christ produces union with all Christ's people, it inevitably follows that *communion* with Christ will also lead to and enrich our communion with our Christian brothers and sisters.

When I was a student I had a very good friend who was studying in the same college. We would meet regularly to pray together. One day, as I was leaving after one of our prayer sessions, I became conscious of the fact that my friend knew nearly everything there was to know about me, as I shared most things about myself with her, but that I knew next to

nothing about her. After considering this for some time I
returned to her room and shared with her my concern that
I had given much of myself to her, while she had kept herself
somewhat closed to me. I explained that I did not expect her
to be as open as I was—we had very different personalities—
but that if we were to continue to be friends, she needed to
share *something* of herself with me, because friendship is a
two-way relationship: a sharing of like minds, a communion
of souls. The Puritan George Swinnock put it like this: 'Next
to communion with God, there is no communion like the
communion of saints.' Jesus told his disciples, 'I have called
you friends, for everything that I learned from my Father I
have made known to you' (John 15:15b). Things did change
with my friend, and I am glad to say that we have remained
friends to this day.

### A 'NO GO' AREA

It is wonderful to have earthly friendships, but to be a
friend of Christ is even more amazing. What intimacy
there is in such a friendship! When no one else understands
us, He does. When we have no one with us, He remains
our constant, faithful companion. Is Christ your closest
friend? At the end of each day, our forefathers would
examine their lives and confess every sin. Short accounts
mattered to them. It is important among friends to learn
to keep these 'short accounts' and always to keep the
channels of communication open; how much more should
that be so with God! We may not share *everything* with
earthly friends, and sometimes it is not wise to do so,
but that should not be the case with the Lord. We must

be willing to share everything with Him: we should not have certain compartments of our lives tucked away from God. Our lives could be compared to a house, each room representing a facet of our being: our married or single state, family, friends, job, ambition, leisure and money. Into how many rooms do we allow the Lord access? We may be willing to share with God our concerns about our family or health, but perhaps we are not so open about the way we spend our money, or the way our pet jealousies affect our fellowship with other members of our church. We may allow Him through the front door of our house, but not into certain rooms tucked away, such as the cellar or the attic (where a lot of 'junk' resides!). These places may stay locked to the One who already knows all there is to know about us and who would willingly commune with us about those marginal things that should not be given room in our lives. Sometimes the Lord has to wait a long time to hear from us. He is often left waiting at the door (Revelation 3:20).

The Holy Spirit continuously searches all our being: what we are before others and what we are in the confines of our homes. He knows us better than we know ourselves. He must have access to everything. When we lock God out, we forfeit communion with Him. We are declaring a 'no go' area to God. But *no entrance* means no entitlement. When our communion with our Saviour is broken, it does not take long before it affects other relationships. All the angst we have with 'our neighbour' can often be traced back to the lack of what Roberts called 'our felt, conscious enjoyment of God's love', His presence in our lives.

## LIVING IN HIS COMPANY

When our communion with Christ is sweet and we know what it is to share everything with Him, then, in our day-to-day sorrows and joys, we can know His comfort and peace. Every moment becomes a conscious living in His company. Christ's desires become our choices. His delight in His people becomes the blessing of fellowship with brothers and sisters. We rejoice in God and in each other; we learn to share our sorrows and joys. One of our desires should be that others around us may enter into this wonderful relationship with the Saviour of sinners, and that they might know the bonds of a close spiritual family. In the society in which we live, so many people know very little about the family unit. There are so many broken homes. One of the saddest things I heard was of a little child remonstrating in the playground with a classmate, saying, 'He was my dad first!'

## TOGETHER IN SORROW

Some time ago, a young woman was converted in our fellowship. She had only been to church a few times in her life, and that as a child. She had said to her partner, 'There must be more to life than this.' Within three weeks of attending church she had found the abundant life that is given to those who seek: she had *union* with Christ. The first time she attended the prayer meeting after her conversion, I really hoped that she would pray so that others would know the same blessing I had received through meeting with her week by week. As the prayer meeting closed, I asked her why she had not taken part. She said, 'Oh, I have so much to learn! You were all praying for other people, and I've only been praying for myself and mine!' The next time we met as a church for prayer, she was among the first to pray. She fervently spoke to God: 'I want to remind You of the Iranian church, and of my dear brother who has been wrongfully imprisoned just for following Christ'—instant *communion* with her Lord, and communion with the saints, both present and at a distance! She had remembered from the last meeting the burden of our prayers at that time. I was extremely moved. Here was a young babe in Christ sharing in Christ's suffering and remembering His *broken* body on earth. She was knowing communion with brothers and sisters of whom she had only very recently learned, and whom she would probably never meet, but for whom she passionately cared. What a wonderful privilege it is to serve one another in this way—but how rarely do we glimpse or grasp these opportunities! How empty some of our prayer meetings are; is that empty seat ours?

Nearly forty years ago, my husband and I were at a memorable meeting that was addressed by a true missionary veteran. The sense of the presence of God in that meeting was so strong that my husband and I were unable to speak to each other until about fifteen minutes after we had left the building. One thing in particular which that dear man of God said has stayed with me: 'Organize a meeting to hear a well-known preacher, and people will come in their bus loads. Organize a prayer meeting across the road for the progress of the gospel in some part of the world, and you may well count those present on your two hands.' Whatever may or may not be true today about the first part of that statement (it was true then), one fears that the second part is as true today as it was nearly forty years ago.

## TOGETHER IN JOY

Communion is sharing with brothers and sisters in times of trouble and *sorrow*, but also in times of *joy*. We can share, also, in Christ's joy as people are saved. In Luke 15:10 we read that 'there is rejoicing in the presence of the angels of God over one sinner who repents'. Jesus did not say that the angels rejoice (though they may well do so); rather, He said that there is rejoicing in their presence. Who is in their presence? God and the souls of saints who have been called home! God and the church triumphant rejoice when one sinner repents.

An Iranian lady began to attend our church some years ago, having asked one of our members with whom she worked if she could go with her. The Iranian woman's home background was very difficult and she felt desperate. It was the difficulty of her situation that led her to begin to seek God. She attended a Bible study I was taking with a number of women, and I distinctly remember her response to the account of Christ's sufferings on the cross and all that this entailed for Him. Glancing at her, I saw that her eyes were brimming with tears, and I knew that she had been affected in some way. Later I discovered that she had had a very real experience of Christ. I asked her to share what had happened.

She had been living in a block of flats with a number of others. One weekend, she knew that all the other women on her floor had gone away. Her sadness was profound and she felt in the very depths of despair. She said that she cried and screamed by turns; then she distinctly heard someone say, 'Be quiet.' She was startled, thinking that someone had slipped back into the complex, so she checked along the corridor; but no, she found the building empty. When she returned to her room and began to cry again, she again heard a voice say quite clearly, 'Be quiet, you are not alone!' With the sound of that voice came an overwhelming sense of peace, and she found herself drawn to read the Bible we had given her. She said, 'Jesus was all around me—He was like the oxygen I breathed. I no longer felt lonely!'

Union and communion! How great should be our rejoicing to know that souls have been set free from the power of sin and that together with them we have been made heirs of salvation! What communion!

But whoever is united with the Lord is one with him in spirit. (1 Corinthians 6:17)

## Food for thought

1. *What is the difference between our* union *and our* communion *with Christ?*
2. *What effects does our lack of communion with God have—on ourselves and on others?*
3. *What is meant by 'keeping short accounts' with God?*
4. *Why might we try to keep certain 'rooms' of our lives closed off from God?*
5. *What does it mean to experience the 'felt, conscious enjoyment of [God's] love'?*

**Note**

1 Roberts, *Great God of Wonders*, p. 42.

# 13 That little word: confession

*If we confess our sins, he is faithful and just and will forgive us
our sins and purify us from all unrighteousness. (1 John 1:9)*

*We are sometimes repentant because of the harm we have
done ourselves and others in our transgressions, but there is
little repentance toward God ... We may regret what our sins
do to our testimony and the evil effect on others, but we are
little concerned because the fellowship with God is broken.
This makes for shallow and inadequate confession because we
have not touched the heart of the trouble. (Vance Havner)*

There is nothing like confession for clearing the atmosphere. We may have had words with our husbands or our children, and there is a stalemate, no one is speaking, and the atmosphere is far from friendly. I remember how, when our children were little, I told them that I was going to teach them a word which was one of the hardest words in the English language but which, if they said it often enough and practised it regularly, would become easier to say. They were mystified when I said that the word had five letters and could only be pronounced in a certain way. Whatever was that word?

## NEED OF SELF-HUMBLING

I am sure you know what that word was, just as I am sure that we have all had the same difficulty saying it on occasion: for it is a word which can only be properly uttered when it truly expresses heartfelt contrition. One cannot say 'sorry' sincerely if one is half-hearted about it, for then it sounds shallow and feeble. Which one of us is going to be the first to say sorry? Who will be first to utter that most difficult little word—difficult because wretched pride in our hearts incapacitates our tongues? Some people never say sorry. They cannot bring themselves to that place of self-humbling without which the word cannot be uttered. Pride, often accompanied with a heavy dose of self-righteousness, has never been taken and strangled, but has been allowed room to grow and has become entrenched in the soul. Sadly, it may even have been diligently nurtured and cultivated like some prized garden plant. Some people can never be seen to be in the wrong. It is a horrible manifestation of pride.

Of course, we are not to say sorry for something we have not done, nor for something that upon scrupulous self-examination we feel could not possibly be perceived as wrong. Sometimes a believer with an over-scrupulous conscience, or one easily intimidated by others and vulnerable to the fear of man (or, worse, the fear of woman!), may say sorry to another person who likes to play the blame game and is utterly oblivious to his or her own faults and failings. This is of no spiritual benefit to the person who says sorry and, sadly, it only confirms the other in the delusion that he or she is in the right. Thus, pride and self-righteousness are fed all the more. Jacob had the truly spiritual attitude. Humbled before the LORD at Peniel, he confessed that he was not worthy of the least of the LORD's mercies (Genesis 32:24–31). But when contending with Laban, he had charged him with the unfair and wrong way in which he had dealt with him (31:38–42).

Spurgeon observed that it was singularly appropriate for Jacob to confess his unworthiness before God, for he really *was* undeserving of God's mercies; but in his dealings with Laban, he *had* earned certain things, and Laban *had* been unjust in his treatment of him.

## FIRST AND MOST EAGER

While pride may make it well-nigh impossible for some people truly to say that they are sorry, we can make it easier for them. Imagine the following situation: we, our husband or our children have eventually said sorry for some misdemeanour, whether by word or action, and the offended party, instead of being conciliatory, says something like 'About time!' Far from pouring oil on troubled waters, this is like emptying petrol upon a smouldering fire! How unhelpful such words are when someone is truly sorry or is attempting reconciliation! How fitting is the Scripture which says, 'Everyone should be quick to listen, slow to speak and slow to become angry, because human anger does not produce the righteousness that God desires' (James 1:19–20). After the word 'sorry', possibly the words 'I forgive you' are the most difficult to say. C. S. Lewis once observed that everybody thinks forgiveness is easy until there is someone they need to forgive. A man once said to John Wesley, 'Sir, I never forgive,' whereupon Wesley wisely replied, 'Then I hope you never sin.' Of all people, those who have been forgiven so much at such tremendous cost—the blood of Christ—by such a great God should be the very first and the most eager to forgive those who have wronged them.

I remember hearing a minister's wife say that there was no way she would ever say sorry to her teenage daughters because she did not intend to be seen by them to be in the wrong. But we should not think we will somehow demean ourselves or lose face by saying sorry to our children. They will learn an important lesson from us: that we are human and, like everyone else, we make mistakes. They are far more likely to listen to us when they know that we are not too proud to admit that we are in the wrong.

D. L. Moody was a powerful and well-known evangelistic preacher. On one occasion a man heckled him during a meeting, and Moody reacted in bad temper. Before the meeting was over he publicly apologized to the man and asked for his forgiveness. Someone who had heard Moody preach many times and who was in the meeting said that it was the greatest thing he had ever seen Moody do or hear him say. Nor was this done simply for effect, in order to be seen to be humble (how pride will sometimes put on the mask of humility as long as it can be allowed to live!). For what Moody did in public before one of his peers, he also did in private before his children. Having seen beautifully manicured lawns in England, he wanted the same kind of thing for himself back in the USA. And so he had a lawn so lovingly cultivated that it could have been used as a bowling green. But his two boys loved football and thought the lawn a wonderful place to practise their skills. Needless to say, the lawn would not have passed muster as a bowling green after their youthful exertions upon his beloved turf! Moody 'lost it' with his two boys. But in bed later that night, they heard his heavy tread upon the stairs. He came into their room and said that the way he had spoken to them was not the way Jesus would have done so. Saying that he had fallen short of the mark of his beloved Master, he expressed his sorrow to his boys and asked for their forgiveness. It was not so much in preaching the gospel to thousands that Moody showed his true greatness, but it was his being willing to humble himself even before his own children and to ask for their forgiveness that he revealed his true spiritual stature. The one who is truly big is small in his or her own eyes and is willing to become as nothing before others. But this spirit and attitude is only possible by first abasing ourselves before God.

### HEAD ABOVE THE PARAPET

God is *always* ready and willing to forgive those who truly repent and confess their sins, and in and through the work of His Son He has devised the wonderful gospel way of granting forgiveness: a way which not only does not sacrifice His justice but which, wonderfully, expresses and displays it. We miss out on so much when we do not confess our sins to the Lord. 'If we confess our sins, he is faithful and just and will forgive us our sins and purify us from all unrighteousness' (1 John 1:9). We can also miss out on much through failing to confess our sins to those whom we have hurt or wronged. Where a relationship—whether in the family, church or elsewhere—has deteriorated and both parties have been at fault, someone has to be willing to put his or her head above the parapet and be the first to apologize, thus beginning the process of restoring peace. How many wasted days or even weeks have we experienced because of our unwillingness to say that we were sorry?

I once heard a true story about a man who, late one Sunday evening, suggested that he and his wife should visit his brother and sister-in-law. His spouse replied that she thought it might not be wise because her sister-in-law would be getting things ready for the children for school the next day. The husband said nothing by way of reply. In fact, he said nothing for the next six months, and thus a stony silence was endured within the family for half a year. Maurice Roberts speaks to such a situation:

> It is the besetting sin of our age to trivialize sin. The remedy is to meditate on the holiness and righteousness of God Himself, on the strictness and perfection of His laws, on the agonies of the damned in hell, and above all, on the sufferings of our blessed Redeemer on the cross of Calvary. The Christian stops making spiritual progress as soon as he stops repenting.[1]

## CROSSING THE GULF

We may find it very difficult to say sorry to one another, but doing so expresses true humility and, in turn, helps to strengthen this Christian virtue and grace. We are not loving others if we refuse to say sorry for some transgression. If someone is unwilling to say sorry to his or her brother or sister, it may call into question how sincere that person's love is for God. 'For whoever does not love their brother and sister, whom they have seen, cannot love God, whom they have not seen' (1 John 4:20). And it follows, of course, that those who are most willing to express contrition to those whom they have wronged are invariably those who are most willing to forgive those who wrong them. The Lord may even test us in order to determine how sincere our love for Him is by seeing how readily we forgive others in obedience to His commands. Bernard of Clairvaux explained that it is essential to make confession, not just to clear our way to God, but also to block up our way from the devil, so that he has no hold over us: 'God removes the sin of the one who makes humble confession, and thereby the devil loses the sovereignty he had gained over the human heart.'[2]

Corrie ten Boom told of a moving incident which occurred at a conference on the theme of forgiveness. At the end of a meeting at which she had been speaking, a man approached her and shared how some years earlier he had been saved. He said that he knew that God had forgiven all his past sins, but he now wished to confess his sin to her and seek *her* forgiveness. As she looked at him her mind went back to her time in a concentration camp during the Second World War, where this very man had not only brutally treated her but had even been the indirect cause of her sister's death. Her arm froze at her side as he extended his hand towards her. How could she ever forgive him? How could he expect this, after all that he had done and all that Corrie and her sister had suffered? Then suddenly into her mind came the words 'If my grace is not big enough to cover his sins, Corrie, then it cannot be big enough to cover yours.' She knew she was being called to be obedient to God's command to 'love your enemies' (Matthew 5:44a) and to 'forgive other people when they sin against you' (6:14a). As she rather reluctantly held out her hand towards the man, something wonderful happened: she felt a sudden surge of love for him filling her heart. Corrie was enabled not only to shake his hand but to throw her arms around him and wholeheartedly embrace him. She knew at that moment that God alone had enabled her to cross that gulf. His love had possessed her and overflowed from her as she simply took that step of obedience to the Lord's commands. I quote again Richard Cecil's description of the drawing power of God's love: 'The union of Christians to Christ, their common head; and by means of the influence they derive from him, one to another, may be illustrated by the loadstone. It not only attracts the particles of iron to itself, by the magnetic virtue, but by this virtue, it unites them one among another.'[3]

## COME TO THE WATERS

It is His grace, His love, His kindness that is known by us and seen in us; we are merely the channel of God's overwhelming goodness to lost mankind. But how often is the flow of Christ's forgiveness, love, comfort and mercy blocked and choked by unconfessed sin or by an unwillingness to forgive sin? 'He committed no sin, and no deceit was found in his mouth' (1 Peter 2:22). We are 100 per cent in the wrong, and He is 100 per cent in the right. The weight of responsibility lies squarely upon our shoulders: we are the guilty party; and the longer we delay confession of our sins to Him, the greater the damage to our communion with God. We lose the sense of the blessed peace of God. So confession is good for the soul and brings us nearer to God; He delights to hear us and desires to forgive us. What comfort to know that He will never refuse to forgive us when we sincerely confess our sins to Him, whatever those sins may be and however deep the pit into which we have fallen. In 1 John 2:1 we are assured of our acceptance in Christ. He will speak on our behalf; we are not alone: 'If anybody does sin, we have an advocate with the Father—Jesus Christ, the Righteous One.' We must constantly remind ourselves of this truth; otherwise our own sinful pride, or the devil, will rob us of that blessing

**HIS TREASURED POSSESSION**

of confession which can lead us to renewed fellowship with God. Maurice Roberts writes very helpfully, '[We must] bring our hearts to God in such a way that we hide nothing from Him . . . We wish to be able to get up from our knees and feel in our consciences that we have exposed ourselves in every way to God. We have laid our very hearts before His gaze.'[4]

When did we last speak to God in that way in confessional prayer? Isaiah 55:1 invites us, 'Come, all you who are thirsty, come to the waters.' We are to come the first time like that, and we are to keep coming for fresh cleansing constantly! When we grieve the Holy Spirit through unconfessed sin, we shatter our fellowship with God. We cannot hope to know Him better until we put things right and tell Him all. How many wasted moments or even years have we let slide? Do we have layer upon layer of unconfessed sin between us and the Lord? If so, we should not be surprised if we feel far from Him. It is quite possible that at times our repentance is made with the wrong motive: our concern can be more for ourselves, of not being thought of badly by others, than for the desire to keep channels flowing freely between us and God. God knows every crevice of our hearts:

We are sometimes repentant because of the harm we have done ourselves and others in our transgressions, but there is little repentance toward God . . . We may regret what our sins do to our testimony and the evil effect on others, but we are little concerned because the fellowship with God is broken. This makes for shallow and inadequate confession because we have not touched the heart of the trouble.[5]

**EVERY CREVICE!**

Can you remember the last time you sincerely confessed your sins to the Lord? If it was some time ago, is there something that is holding you back from the full and free confession you should rightly make? Do you perhaps feel bitter against God because of the way He has led you, where He has placed you, or how He has dealt with you? All His dealings with His children are in love and for their good. It is the devil who misrepresents God to us. We are to remember to look up, not down. The devil would have us earth-bound, whereas our hearts should be set 'on things above' (Colossians 3:1).

**THE WRONG PREMISE**

I remember, as a very young Christian, having the following dream which has stayed with me throughout my life. It reminded me of God's willingness to be there even when we feel our strength has gone and we cannot pray. God can *read* our hearts.

I was walking between a long narrow avenue of trees; I seemed to have been walking for mile after mile. As I was drawing closer to the end of the road I could see a figure in the distance who was approaching me. As he drew close I could see it was the devil. I stopped in my tracks, and as he came nearer and nearer my legs grew weaker until they could hardly support me. I could not move; I was terrified! As he approached me and was about to grab hold of me I sank down in terror; but as I fell backwards I was forced to look up. There above me was my blessed Lord looking down with the most wonderful smile upon His face! His reassurance gave me new strength; and Christ's appearance was sufficient to send the devil fleeing back down the path along which he had come.[6]

We are never to allow the devil to keep us from God. Satan will tell us all manner of things to prevent us from coming to Him: that our sin is too great; we have come with the same sin too many times; God cannot forgive us again; we have lost touch with God; we are not real Christians; our prayers do not reach higher than the ceiling—and on and on. We can come even when we feel at our worst and at our lowest: the scandal of the cross is that we can come at any time, in any condition. What are we really saying if we feel we cannot come to God because of how bad we feel? It means that we come at other times because we feel we have merit! In that case, we are coming on the wrong premise. Every time we come to God it must be as we did at first, with nothing in our hands, simply clinging to Christ. The Spirit pinpoints our sin to make us holy, not to destroy us or to rub our noses in the dirt. By contrast, Satan wants to smash us and see us grovelling on the ground. We need to be aware of his methods: the devil is destructive in his dealings with us, whereas the Lord's way with us is constructive. We may not be able to answer the devil, but we have One who can. Flee to Him! Hide in Him (Proverbs 18:10)! Confess all to Him!

### MAJOR OR MINOR KEY?

Christ, not the devil, should have centre stage in our lives. Have we allowed Satan or things or other people to usurp Christ's central place? Is the Lord the priority of our lives, or is He very much known in the minor key? Philippians 3:8 tells us how we should view our relationship with Christ: 'I consider everything a loss because of the surpassing worth of knowing Christ Jesus my Lord, for whose sake I have lost all things.' Do we view our reputation, our popularity, our prosperity, and an immensely long list of other things that fill our lives, as less than nothing in comparison with the amazing fact of knowing Christ? If this is not the case, we do not have the same desire to know Christ that Paul had. The apostle affirms in that wonderful letter to the Philippians, 'I consider them rubbish, that I may gain Christ and be found in him' (3:8). Paul wanted not only to know Christ, but much, much more: 'I want to know Christ—yes, to know the power of his resurrection and participation in his sufferings, becoming like him in his death' (3:10). Do we know anything of Christ in His resurrection: knowing what it is day by day to put to death our sin by *confessing* our need, and fleeing to Him for refuge and forgiveness?

I prayed to the LORD my God and confessed: 'Lord, the great and awesome God, who keeps his covenant of love with those who love him and keep his commandments, we have sinned and done wrong . . . Lord, listen! Lord, forgive!' (Daniel 9:4–5a, 19a)

## Food for thought

1. *Do you find it difficult to say sorry? What may be the reasons why we sometimes don't want to confess we are in the wrong?*

2. *Why is it not helpful to say sorry when we are not at fault?*

3. *What does the regular confession of sin nurture in us?*

4. *What is God's response to those who will not forgive others?*

**HIS TREASURED POSSESSION**

*5. How does the devil try to keep us from God?*

*6. Do 'things' have a greater place in our lives than Christ?*

**Notes**

1  Roberts, *Thought of God*, p. 12.

2  Bernard, 'Sermon 6'.

3  Cecil, *Remains*, p. 249.

4  Roberts, *Great God of Wonders*, p. 14.

5  Havner, *Chosen Path*, p. 29.

6  Note 1 Peter 5:8–9a: 'Be alert and of sober mind. Your enemy the devil prowls around like a roaring lion looking for someone to devour. Resist him, standing firm in the faith.'

# 14 The passive side: contemplation

*May these words of my mouth and this meditation of my heart*
  *be pleasing in your sight,*
  *Lord, my Rock and my Redeemer.*
*(Psalm 19:14)*

*The reason we come away so cold from reading*
*the word is because we do not warm ourselves at*
*the fire of meditation. (Thomas Watson)*

Contemplation,[1] or meditation (as it is more commonly known), is largely a lost art in our busy modern world. American pastor Vance Havner loathed busyness and noise, preferring solitude and simplicity. He suggested, 'It is high time we learned that in this nerve-wrecking, maddening modern rush, we have let the spirit of the times rob us utterly of meditation, devotion, rest, the passive side of our Christian experience, without which we cannot be truly active to the glory of God.'[2]

We need to be reminded of this lost practice. The Scriptures are full of encouragement for us to pursue this 'passive activity' with great diligence. I must confess that, until I started to contemplate (!) this subject, I did not realize just how many verses there are in the Bible that refer to it. In the New Testament there is support for this pursuit in Philippians 4:8: 'Whatever is true, whatever is noble, whatever is right, whatever is pure, whatever is lovely, whatever is admirable—if anything is excellent or praiseworthy—*think about such things.*' Then Colossians 3:1 directs us to '*Set your hearts on things above*, where Christ is, seated at the right hand of God.' We are also told that 'Mary treasured up all these things and *pondered* them in her heart' (Luke 2:19). Jesus taught that we should 'look at the birds' (Matthew 6:26) and 'consider the ravens' (Luke 12:24–26). Then we are to note the flowers of the field and even the little hyraxes (conies), who live in the crags.[3] We find the same sentiment in many of the psalms. Also, in Joshua 1:8 God tells Joshua to 'Keep this Book of the Law always on your lips; *meditate* on it day and night, so that you may be careful to do everything written in it.' We can even contemplate things that have not yet been (1 Corinthians 2:9–10).

We could go on and on, but these few examples should convince us of the importance of contemplating the magnificence of all that is ours in Christ our Lord. And since, as Paul tells us in 1 Corinthians 3:21, all things are ours, our meditation upon all that is ours in Christ will include thinking of God's great works in creation and His great work in the new creation—both His work of grace now, and the time when that work is completed ('Finish, then, Thy new creation').[4] Further instruction is given by one of the great Puritan writers, Thomas Brooks:

Remember, it is not hasty reading—but serious meditating upon holy and heavenly truths, that make them prove sweet and profitable to the soul. It is not the bee's touching of the flower, which gathers honey—but her abiding for a time upon the flower, which draws out the sweet. It is not he who reads most—but he who meditates most, who will prove the choicest, sweetest, wisest and strongest Christian.[5]

## PASSING ON THE BATON

Was this Spurgeon's secret? He said of prayer that he had never prayed for more than twenty minutes at one time, but that there was never a period longer than twenty minutes when he was not praying. By this reckoning, most of Spurgeon's day was spent in prayer and meditation. This wonderfully demonstrates the superlative art of contemplation! It has been said that 'prayer is talking to God, and meditating is listening to God'. So many great men and women of God incorporated this into their lives. And as we read of their spiritual practices, we must remember that these godly people did not record them to draw attention to themselves, but to be of help and an encouragement to us. They were passing on the baton so that the blessings they knew might be known and enjoyed by another generation; so that we, with like faith, might be encouraged in our souls to integrate such practices into our lives, as helps to further holiness. Spurgeon said,

How many of you meditate on Christ? Christian men and women, do not many of you live below your privileges? Are you not living without having choice moments of communion with your Savior? I think if you had a free pass to Heaven's palace, you would use it very often. If you might go there whenever you liked and hold communion with some person whom you dearly loved, you would often be found there. But here is your blessed Lord Jesus, the King of Heaven, and He gives you that which can admit you to intimate communion with Him! And yet you live without meditating upon His work, meditating upon His Person, meditating upon His offices, and meditating upon His Glory.[6]

## COME TO THE TABLE

Do we enjoy Christ's company? 'The proof of the pudding is in its eating,' as the saying goes. Do we regularly come to the table? To change the metaphor, have we not found that, if we are married and have children, if we have been away from our husbands or children for any length of time, we have a longing to hear their voices, receive a letter or text message, or any other form of communication, that will bring us closer to them? Most people find it difficult if they are away from their loved ones for any length of time and have no contact with them—especially if those loved ones are never thinking about them or remembering shared special or even ordinary events. Such absence and lack of communication soon leads to deterioration in the relationship. Is this what happens to us when we do not contemplate God and all He has done for us in Jesus Christ? Is he like a 'wayfaring man'[7] who turns aside and only tarries for a night, always sent away from 'home'? Do we only meditate upon the Lord now and again, perhaps when something jogs our memory?

## AT ANY TIME OR ANYWHERE

At this point we could be boarding the wagon for a guilt trip. So it is important to recognize that some people are far more contemplative than others, and that meditation comes far more naturally to some than to others because of their personalities or circumstances. There are those who are naturally meditative, while others are far more active.

I remember a man once telling me that for every gram of activity, he would spend a kilo on meditation. 'In fact,' he said, 'I would often wear myself into the ground by thinking. I didn't enjoy being with people too often because it deprived me of time to meditate!' An active person, of course, would never have this problem; but whatever our temperament, we should always be in control of it, instead of letting it control us.

For both the contemplative and the active person there are occasionally legitimate times in our lives when we are not able to *commune* with God in the way that we wish. We may be busy with babies and children, or with parents and grandchildren. But these very occasions—when feeding the baby, or when caring for older folk—may be the times when the art of *contemplation* can be employed. Wherever we are, whatever we are doing, even during the busiest of times, our thoughts can turn to the Lord: while we are doing routine shopping, cleaning, or a thousand and one other things for which we do not have to concentrate, our minds can be taken up with God. Some quite naturally flood their minds with music, and others may have a melodious voice and enjoy singing, but there are surely times when it is good for us to introduce this waning, if not 'foreign', art of contemplation.

We may sometimes be guilty of using our activity as an excuse for not having time: we are involved in ministry and/ or secular work and we never seem to have the time to nurture more than a fleeting relationship with the Lord. But there was no busier man than George Müller, and in his autobiography he shared something of his daily practice:

The most important thing I had to do was to give myself to
the reading of the Word of God and to meditation on it, that
thus my heart might be comforted, encouraged, warned,
reproved, instructed; and that thus, whilst meditating, my
heart might be brought into experimental communion with the
Lord . . . for the sake of obtaining food for my own soul.[8]

## ABOVE ALL, DISCIPLINE

In the midst of all the things that daily clamoured for
his attention, he fitted in that *discipline* of the art of
contemplation, which comes with practice. So for us: Christ,
in this way, can become our constant companion. Our
thoughts can be taken up with Him—in contact, communion,
confession—and in our steadfast contemplation of Him we
will go on to *know* the Lord in greater depth and reality.
This was Christ's pattern when He walked this earth: He
was in constant communion with and contemplation of His
heavenly Father. May it also be ours!

May my meditation be pleasing to him,
as I rejoice in the LORD. (Psalm 104:34)

## Food for thought

1. *What 'things' is it helpful to contemplate?*
2. *Is Christ like a 'wayfaring man' to you? What does that term mean?*
3. *What bearing does temperament have on the whole subject of contemplation?*
4. *Are there periods in our lives when contemplation could be difficult? How can we help ourselves during these times?*

**HIS TREASURED POSSESSION**

**Notes**

1  I use the term 'contemplation' rather than 'meditation' in this chapter in order to make it easier to remember the headings of the chapters in this section, many of which begin with the letter 'C'.

2  Havner, *Chosen Path*, p. 35.

3  Proverbs 30:24 speaks of 'four things on earth [that] are small, yet they are extremely wise': ants, hyraxes, locusts and lizards. How often have we contemplated these little creatures?

4  From Charles Wesley, 'Love Divine, All Loves Excelling'.

5  Brooks, *Precious Remedies*, pp. 21–22.

6  Spurgeon, 'Meditation on God', Sermon no. 2690, Christian Classics Ethereal Library, https://www.ccel.org/ccel/spurgeon/sermons46.xxxv.html.

7  'Wayfaring Man': 'The translation in Judges 19:17; 2 Samuel 12:4; Jeremiah 9:2; Jeremiah 14:8 of (*'oreach*), the participle of *'arach*, "to journey". In Isaiah 33:8 of *'obher 'orach*, "one passing on a path", and in Isaiah 35:8 of *holekh derekh*, "one walking on a road". "Traveller" is the meaning in all cases.' From *International Standard Bible Encyclopedia*, quoted at BibleHub, https://biblehub.com/topical/w/wayfaring.htm.

8  Müller, *Autobiography*, pp. 152–153.

# 15 A new dimension: my soul

*Dear friends, I urge you, as foreigners and exiles, to abstain from sinful desires, which wage war against your soul. (1 Peter 2:11)*

*If God declares that all is well, ten thousand devils may declare it to be ill, but we laugh them all to scorn. Blessed be God for a faith which enables us to believe God when the creatures contradict Him. (C. H. Spurgeon)*

Over the last few chapters we have looked at our desire to know God, and at ways to help us in our pursuit of knowing Him more deeply and experientially. We now turn to the desire *to know our souls*. To put it simply, the soul is the essence of our being; it is who we are. Since Adam's fall into sin, humanity is naturally evil, and our souls are necessarily polluted by sin. In new birth God implants a principle of new spiritual life within us. This begins in us the work of moral and spiritual renovation. This means, therefore, that in one sense we are already saved. Although this is so, we do not yet have full salvation. This already/not yet tension is to be seen in many New Testament passages, and it is something of which we become acutely aware. For although we are now new people in Christ, the fact remains that sin—and, therefore, its polluting effects—remains within us. Thus, there is a battle. This is why J. C. Ryle could say that the true Christian is characterized as much by inner conflict—that is, against sin—

as by inner peace. Getting to know ourselves, therefore, is an essential part of the process of godliness. If we do not know ourselves, we will not be able to tackle those areas of our lives which constantly drag us down in our quest for holiness and our desire to be transformed into Christ's likeness.

## SERIOUS CONSIDERATION

I recall the first time I consciously noticed the word 'soul' being used. It was the night after I had become a Christian. Although I had met with the Lord in the quiet of my bedroom, I had not grasped or understood all that had happened and did not realize at the time that 'the great work' had begun in me. The next evening I went with my sister to a baptismal service at a local church. She had been invited to this particular church some weeks earlier and had come to faith in Christ at that time; as a result, she had begun to get to know the minister of the church. He was a man possessed with a true burden for people to be brought to faith in Christ. I was deeply affected by the hymns that we sang: I realized that I was the sinner of which they spoke. The message also had a profound effect upon me, for the Saviour of sinners was powerfully proclaimed and He shone through. It was here for the first time that I truly heard of all that Christ had done for sinners and realized that He had done it for me. I remember my sister asking if I wanted to speak with the minister. Without really thinking, I said, 'Yes,' but I did not know what I was going to say to him, and I more or less told him that when he asked me what was wrong. It was apparent to all that I was distressed. The minister took me by the hand

and said to the congregation, 'This young woman has *soul* trouble.'

## ONE MOST IMPORTANT THING

It was not until later, looking back, that I realized that I had probably in fact been saved the night before. As a young Christian I soon grasped that there was now a new dimension to my life. One of the things of which I had become aware was that I had, or was, a living soul. I had hitherto been ignorant of this, but from that moment my soul was something I had seriously to consider. Very soon after I became a Christian I needed no one to tell me that there was an actual devil, for he very quickly made his presence felt! I am grateful that very early on in my Christian experience I was taught that the most important thing for me to do was to keep looking to God. 'Truly my soul finds rest in God; my salvation comes from him' (Psalm 62:1). J. I. Packer expresses this point most helpfully: 'Once you become aware that the main business that you are here for is to know God, most of life's problems fall into place of their own accord.'[1]

God is like the centre of a wheel; He is the 'hub', right in the middle. If He is truly at the centre of our lives, every aspect of what we say and do will radiate from that centre. Just as the spokes of a wheel go from the hub to its circumference, so God touches every avenue and 'spoke' of our lives, and this, in turn, affects and touches those with whom we come into contact. Moreover, every aspect of our being is affected by being in communion with God: the physical, emotional, psychological and spiritual aspects; and the private as well as the social and interpersonal realms.

For you created my inmost being;
  you knit me together in my mother's womb.
I praise you because I am fearfully and wonderfully made;
  your works are wonderful,
    I know that full well.
My frame was not hidden from you
    when I was made in the secret place,
    when I was woven together in the depths of the earth.
Your eyes saw my unformed body;
    all the days ordained for me were written in your book
    before one of them came to be. (Psalm 139:13–16)

## Food for thought

 1. *What does it mean to 'know our souls'?*

 2. *Do you allow God into every area of your life?*

 3. *Do you take the devil seriously? Are you conscious of the devil seeking to bind you to this world?*

 4. *Are you aware of weaknesses in certain areas of your life, and that the devil seeks to use these as a 'landing ground'?*

 6. *Do you guard yourself against temptation, and take precautions to limit your exposure to it?*

**Note**

**1**  Packer, *Knowing God*, p. 31.

# 16 Close and personal: dependence on God

*For I am the LORD your God*
  *who takes hold of your right hand*
*and says to you, Do not fear;*
  *I will help you. (Isaiah 41:13)*

*God desired to reveal Himself in and through His creatures*
*by communicating to them as much of His own goodness and*
*glory as they were capable of receiving. But this communication*
*was not meant to give created beings something they could*
*possess in themselves, having full charge and access apart*
*from Him. Rather, God as the ever-living, ever-present,*
*ever-acting One, who upholds all things by the word of*
*His power, and in whom all things exist, meant that the*
*relationship of His creatures to Himself would be one of*
*unceasing, absolute dependence. As truly as God by His*
*power once created all things, so by that same power must*
*God every moment maintain all things. (Andrew Murray)*

Many people would imagine that if a man were to have a top-rate job, live in a mansion with a servant to take care of all his needs, have well-connected friends and all his requirements met by the bank, where he had vast wealth deposited, that man would be living life with a capital L. 'What a life!' they would say. But now envisage that man experiencing the loss of his job, and living in a country with no government handouts and no one prepared to do anything to help him, so that within a very short time he is out on the streets, having to beg in order to survive. In addition to all this, imagine that the little he owned and had not had to sell was taken by vagrants amongst whom he was forced to live. That man would be absolutely destitute, and more miserable than he had ever been before in his life. What a contrast to his former way of life! What unbelievable heartache and sadness for that soul, after such riches and abundance, to be now in the depths of despair and poverty!

Now imagine that that man, who has fallen so far and is now living rough, is approached by someone of whom he has only vaguely heard, someone who makes a remarkable, life-changing offer. The 'rescuer' says that he intends to buy the mansion the destitute man once lived in and renovate the whole building. He will take him to a spa for a thorough clean-up, after which he will provide a new set of top-quality designer clothes for the man to wear. Then, as if all this were not enough, awaiting the man would be a dinner in a Michelin-starred restaurant. In addition, he could return to his former place of work, but with the following changes: the company is now housed in a brand-new complex, and the generous benefactor, who is none other than the chairman of the company, wants to give him a place on the board! You could be quite sure that the man would be overjoyed and filled with gratitude towards his benefactor, feeling a sense of obligation to him for the rest of his life—an obligation of love rather than of cold duty—and surely giving of his very best to his work.

We would undoubtedly, therefore, be saddened and shocked to learn that within a very short period of joining the board, the man begins to take everything for granted,

**HIS TREASURED POSSESSION**

adopting a 'couldn't care less' attitude to the man who has placed his life on a new and secure foundation.

Sadly, though, this may often—alas! all too often—be a picture of the Christian. Having lost so much 'in Adam', we need to remember the wretched mess from which we were taken and the One who lifted us up, and how and why He did so:

You were dead in your transgressions and sins, in which
you used to live when you followed the ways of this world
and of the ruler of the kingdom of the air, the spirit who is
now at work in those who are disobedient. All of us also
lived among them at one time, gratifying the cravings of our
flesh and following its desires and thoughts. Like the rest,
we were by nature deserving of wrath. (Ephesians 2:1–3)

God, in His great mercy, opened our eyes to see how spiritually poor and wretched we really were:

He lifted me out of the slimy pit,
    out of the mud and mire;
he set my feet on a rock
    and gave me a firm place to stand. (Psalm 40:2)

'The Rescuer'—the Lord Jesus Christ—gave us an absolutely brand-new life: taking away our filth and degradation, giving us His spotless robe of righteousness, providing us with a banquet, inviting us to be co-workers with Him in His work here on earth. What loyalty we should render Him! What heartfelt gratitude should be ours throughout our whole lives! How privileged and thankful we should feel to be working for such a Saviour!

## LITTLE CONCERN?

But is this our response, or have we become like the man in the story? At first we were conscious of our privileges; at one time we daily remembered the blessings that had been undeservedly showered upon us. But now? Are we taking for granted all the pain, suffering and agony that it cost our Saviour to procure this new life for us? Do we show little care or concern for our Saviour, who saved us so that we could be in partnership with Him and do His work? God forbid that we should be so heartless! God forbid that we should forget how much we have for which to thank Him! And God forbid that we should be empty of praise and gratitude! 'Therefore, . . . in view of God's mercy, [let us] offer [our] bodies as a living sacrifice, holy and pleasing to God—this is [our] true and proper worship' (Romans 12:1). May it be that, when we appear before Him, the Lord will be able to say, 'Well done, good and faithful servant! . . . Come and share your master's happiness!' (Matthew 25:23), and we will avoid the censure He gave to the rich farmer: 'You fool! This very night your life will be demanded from you. Then who will get what you have prepared for yourself?' (Luke 12:20). I am sure we would far prefer to be called 'faithful servants' than 'fools': all the work in between will be so worthwhile if we could hear those blessed words from our Saviour.

## NOTHING, ABSOLUTELY NOTHING!

Let us again ask ourselves the question Augustine was asked: 'What do you desire?' Earthly fame and fortune? Or is it to walk in utter dependence on God? If it is the latter, a sure way of showing just how dependent we are on the Lord is to stay close to Him. The attitude of the world in which we live is one of self-help, self-importance and self-gratification: self, self, self is the order of the day. We have to break radically from this mindset and remind ourselves, day by day, that 'apart from me you can do nothing' (John 15:5b). And that means exactly what it says: nothing, absolutely nothing! When we learn that lesson we are in a good place, because then we will learn to pray about everything.

Someone said to me recently, 'Oh, I couldn't pray about that, it's too trivial.' Would a best friend really say something was too trivial to listen to or to share? If someone is truly our friend, that person will want to be part of anything and everything that relates to us. We may not always be personally interested in what our loved ones want to tell us—they may have very different interests from ours—but because we love them we want them to feel that they can share anything. We are there to rejoice with them in their joys and to commiserate with them when they are sad. Do we fully appreciate the fact that God is always interested in us? He always wants us to be aware that He is there, with His immense love, to support and sustain us through our happy and sad times. It is we who lose out when we forget how dependent upon Him we are for everything. The privilege is ours that we are able to lean upon Him, upon whose shoulders the government of all rests.

### WHY STRUGGLE?

My mother-in-law was an amazingly independent woman, although registered blind. And there were times, when she lived with us, when she would try to do many things of which she knew she was incapable. It was both sad and yet sometimes comical to see how much she struggled to do things for herself. She either gave up in utter frustration or, as often happened, I would have to wrench things from her in order to help her. How often we are like that with God! He has promised to assist us and to give us all we need to live holy lives, but we still continue to struggle along in our own weakness. When will we ever learn to lean upon Him? We will always be in need of God in a much deeper way than a small child is in need of its parent(s). And this will be so for the whole of our lives. And just as it is appropriate for children or grandchildren to express thankfulness to their parents or grandparents for a kindness or a gift, so we too need to show and express our thankfulness to our great and glorious God, in prayer and by living to please Him. We shall always be His beloved children.

## SUSTAINING POWER

I remember seeing a poster outside a church that deeply challenged me: 'If you only had today the things you thanked God for yesterday, what would they be?' Are we in the habit of thanking God for small blessings as well as great ones? A parent may feel deep pleasure when a little child expresses its trust in and dependence upon him or her. However, as the child grows and matures, it becomes less dependent. Here is one great difference between maturity in the natural and in the spiritual realm: we are *always* dependent upon our heavenly Father, and spiritual maturity consists partly in an ever-deepening awareness of this. When we live close to Him and learn consciously to depend upon Him, we will have that vital contact with God, regular communication with

Him, and we shall make confession and be in the habit of contemplating all the great attributes of our God. And thus, being aware of all our needs, we will know God's sustaining power keeping us.

Those who hope in the LORD
 will renew their strength.
They will soar on wings like eagles;
 they will run and not grow weary,
 they will walk and not be faint. (Isaiah 40:31)

## Food for thought

1. *Are you daily conscious of a heartfelt gratitude to God for your salvation?*
2. *Are you aware of how much you need God? Are you consciously dependent on Him?*
3. *Will God regard you as a 'fool' or a 'faithful servant' when you appear before Him?*
4. *What are you seeking in this world? Is it earthly fame and fortune, or to walk in dependence upon God?*
5. *Do you tell God how much you need Him? Do you thank God daily for all He gives you?*

# 17 Constant refining: weaknesses and strengths

*We are the clay, you are the potter;*
*we are all the work of your hand. (Isaiah 64:8)*

*How can we possibly believe the promises concerning Heaven,*
*immortality, and glory, when we do not believe the promises*
*concerning our present life? And how can we be trusted when we*
*say we believe these promises but make no effort to experience*
*them ourselves? It is just here that men deceive themselves. It*
*is not that they do not want the Gospel privileges of joy, peace*
*and assurance, but they are not prepared to repent of their evil*
*attitudes and careless life-styles. Some have even attempted to*
*reconcile these things and ruined their souls. (John Owen)*

Have you ever found yourself thanking God that you were not born in a certain century or in a particular nation, or that you were not born to certain parents, or did not live in a particular town or city? When, where and to whom we were born have great significance for the way we live. Why is it that we were not born, for example, in the nineteenth century in Tierra del Fuego in South America, where a tribe wore no clothes, regardless of the season, and the menfolk, children included, killed their womenfolk to survive the winters? Many of the elderly women who tried to escape into the mountains were dragged back to the village and held over a smoking fire until they choked to death. Or why were we not born amongst the young children who eke out an existence rummaging through refuse on the ash heaps of Manila in the Philippines? Into the mix of century, birthplace and family we can add other factors: our surroundings, the people who have crossed our paths and influenced our lives, the jobs we have had or not had—the list could go on endlessly.

For the Christian, the answer to these questions lies in the belief that God is sovereign over all things and circumstances; He is the wonderful anchorage point. Knowing Him, and that He is in control of all these factors, helps us to cope with disappointments, dashed hopes, glaring mistakes, unbelievable hardships, or wrecked and sullied relationships. When our lives centre upon our supreme God, who 'chose us in him before the creation of the world to be holy in his sight' (Ephesians 1:4), we have the ballast we need to help us deal with the multitude of circumstances that face us in our short, uncertain lives. We can face our strengths and weaknesses, knowing that we are not on our own.

What an amazing and comforting thought: God knows everything about all our weaknesses and strengths that have found expression through us in our little corner of the world! He formed us and placed us where we are; He knows the soil in which we will grow best. Instead of being slaves to the way we are, and to the areas of our lives that cause us pain, we can confront them and find strength and help to deal with them. The wonderful and encouraging thing is that, although our strengths, as well as our weaknesses, can lead us to stumble, we have God on our side now to help us control our temperament.

## NO SHADOWS

Weaknesses in character vary from person to person: we may have a tendency to lie, swear, covet, think badly of people, be unkind or ungenerous. We need to deal with these weak and sinful areas of our lives; we must not allow them to live in our hearts. 'Do you not know that your bodies are temples of the Holy Spirit, who is in you?' (1 Corinthians 6:19). Darkness should not be allowed to creep into the light: we want no shadows in our spiritual lungs!

On the other hand, our strengths should be cultivated: we may be long-suffering, patient, dependable, considerate or trustworthy. If so, we should strengthen and develop these virtues. We are in constant need of being refined. Our very strengths can, though, in some cases become our weaknesses. Remember Peter, so sure of himself, so confident that he, of all the disciples, would not fail the Lord. Yet it was his zeal and readiness to avow his love for Christ which was the occasion of his undoing and of his denial of his Lord. The reason for this was his inability to realize his own weakness and, therefore, his failure to watch and pray.

## A TIGHT REIN

Spurgeon is a wonderful example of a man who knew both his strengths and his weaknesses. God had blessed him with a wonderful sense of humour. This was something which, by grace, was sanctified and refined and used in his Master's service. Many a man has abused such a gift, cheapening and trivializing God's truth and taking away from the sobriety and seriousness which should ever characterize our approach to the things of God. Spurgeon was well aware of this danger. The result was that he kept this area under control. His sermons demonstrate again and again that he employed this gift to good effect. As he once put it, 'I tickle my oysters to open them and then put in the knife!' He once referred to a comment that had been made about another preacher. One hearer had complained to another that the preacher made people laugh. This met with the reply: 'Yes, but he also made them weep for their sins.' Spurgeon heartily approved. When one of Spurgeon's own hearers expressed criticism to him of the amount of humour in his sermons, Spurgeon— ever humble and conscious of his own failings—replied that perhaps his critic had a point. But he then went on to say that if the man had realized how much humour he was leaving out of his sermons, he would have given him more credit! In other words, Spurgeon kept a tight rein on himself, knowing that one of his strengths could easily become a weakness and thereby limit his spiritual usefulness.

## GETTING READY FOR GLORY

God's plan for us often involves placing us in difficult situations where we will be able to grow; but when faced with difficult circumstances we often want to give up, not seeing the purpose behind them. When one of my sons was quite young, whenever he was confronted with a situation he found irksome I would say to him that God was using the circumstances to build his character. On one occasion, before I had a chance to say anything, he said, 'I think I've had enough of this character building!' He may have been allowed to say that as a child, but as adults we should learn to say, 'God knows best!' We need constantly to remind ourselves that He is getting us ready for glory, and experiencing trials, although painful at the moment, 'produces a harvest of righteousness and peace for those who have been trained by it' (Hebrews 12:11b).

Something that will exercise you may not exercise me, and vice versa. We all need our individual workouts. My husband has often claimed that every traffic light he drives towards turns red just before he gets there, or that he is always the first to arrive at a traffic light when it is red. At first I thought he was exaggerating, but I have too often been a witness of the fact to dispute it. I have suggested that maybe he needs to learn patience in this area, and that red lights are his exercise 'weights' for the day. He, in turn, can point to the fact that I become impatient with tailbacks on the motorway and constantly want to change lanes rather than stay where I am. (He is undoubtedly right in saying that each lane has a spurt of movement before coming to a halt.) My turn to visit the gym! We all have weaknesses and strengths in our temperaments and in the way we react to different situations. God brings certain areas to our attention, and we would do well to acknowledge those parts of our lives that need to be addressed. Thomas Watson reassures us:

To know that nothing hurts the godly, is a matter of comfort; but to be assured that all things which fall out shall co-operate for their good, that their crosses shall be turned into blessings, that showers of affliction water the withering root of their grace and make it flourish more; this may fill their hearts with joy till they run over.[1]

## CONTEND, NOT BEND

Oh that it were quite so easy to recognize that each 'cross' has been kindly delivered in order for us to grow! We may, for example, resent a well-intentioned comment from a kind spouse pointing out a particular weakness, whereas we should welcome it as a help to our growth in grace. In responding to words of exhortation, we need to take account of our own sinfulness and the sinful actions and reactions around us; and into that mix we need to reckon with the constant presence of our arch-enemy, the devil, who knows our weaknesses and strengths inside out. That makes for an extremely potent mix! If we do not contend, we will simply bend—to the way we want to go, not to the way God desires us to go. God wants our cooperation as he seeks to transform our characters, so that we are changed from one degree of glory to another. It is a lifelong process, and it will not end 'till in heaven we take our place'.[2] So we need to determine to be as teachable as we can be when being exercised in God's school.

### THE DEVIL'S WHISPERS

God wants our good, and He helps and supports us in our conflicts. The devil is no friend of ours, though he masquerades as one. God builds; the devil pulls down. If we constantly find ourselves feeling crushed, we need to assure ourselves of this: God never seeks to demoralize us, but wants to help us and equip us. The devil loves to 'nag', using non-specific accusations, or pointing out things of which we have long since repented. He seeks constantly to point out our weaknesses. He will continually drive us to one of two extremes. Like Peter, we may believe that we can do anything and everything in our own strength. Of this the great Puritan Stephen Charnock wrote, 'A proud faith is as much a contradiction as a humble devil.' Alternatively, we may feel that we can do nothing, even with the help of God! The devil whispers that we are useless, that we have never done anything of any significance for God, and that we are never likely to do so. He will point out individuals we know and parade their abilities and accomplishments, and anything else that suits this specific onslaught. We need to resist him because ultimately it is not what we do, or do not do, that counts. Horatius Bonar declared in a hymn, 'Upon a life I did not live, upon a death I did not die; another's life, another's death, I stake my whole eternity.' When we grasp our high calling in Christ and contemplate His power in us, it changes the whole of our lives. It is not what we can do, but what *He* can do through us: such knowledge transforms. When we realize that all we do is done *by* God, *with* God and *for* God, it can take away all the stress and strain of living.

## 'I LOVE THE WAY GOD MADE YOU'

When my husband was first in the ministry, things were not at all easy. I am sure that the stress and strain we knew at that time contributed to a period of depression in my life. My doctor diagnosed that I was suffering from a hormonal imbalance. I remember it was about this time that we were invited to spend a holiday with the family of an old university friend of my husband's. These friends were very able intellectually and very capable musicians. In my depressed state of mind at the time, I barely managed to survive the week away with them. I can remember telling my husband at the end of the week that I would not be going on holiday again with these friends (they were already planning for the following year). Although I knew that I was depressed, I was unable to grasp how this contributed to the way I felt about myself and to the way in which the devil exploited the situation. I felt overwhelmed by all my failures and weaknesses. I remember thinking that I was hopeless company, that I could not cook like my friend, that I was a failure at board games—I will not bore you with all the details. Suffice it to say, I had determined that I would never spend another holiday with these dear friends![3]

On the morning of our departure I was left alone at the breakfast table with my youngest son, who was just four years old at the time, while everyone else packed their cases. I was buried in my thoughts when my little boy touched my hand and, not knowing anything about how I was feeling, simply said, 'Mummy, I love the way God made you,' and then just went on eating his breakfast as if he had not been party to what he had said! I wanted to cry because I knew that it was God who had spoken to me. I felt frozen in time; it was as if He had shaken me and said, 'I've made you as you are, so your quarrel is with Me. I don't want you to try to be like others—all my children are unique. I have made you for Myself.' I cannot begin to describe what I felt that morning. I know that above all there was release from a crippling sense of failure; I felt as though I had been set free. I did not need to compare myself with anyone else in the world. I was His, and He was mine,[4] just as I was, for ever and ever. It was so insightful it was like a second conversion.

**HIS TREASURED POSSESSION**

## NOT IN COMPETITION

I had been hankering to be like other people, not content with the way God had made me. I felt so ashamed. Since that day I have never craved other people's gifts but sought to thank God for the many gifted people He has given to His church. 'But God has put the body together, giving greater honour to the parts that lacked it, so that there should be no division in the body, but that its parts should have equal concern for each other' (1 Corinthians 12:24b–25). If we but realize that we are not in competition but, by God's grace, complement one another, there can be a sense of partnership amongst us, not rivalry; the latter belongs to the old nature. We can each offer something unique to God's church. We need to ask Him to use our strengths and refine our weaknesses.

## THE RIGHT SHAPE

When a house is being built, it is no good having twenty carpenters and just one bricklayer! So it is with God's church; although it needs constant renovation, He has made the structure solid because Christ is the foundation: His church will never fall. And He has made the stones just the right shape to fit into the building. So when we are tempted to look around and think, 'If only I had their gifts, or their home, or their family,' we should remember that it is Christ who has made us, primarily for Himself, and then for one another.

This reminds me of a dream someone recounted to me. There were a number of people standing in a line, and Christ passed by each of them; hugging one, kissing another, touching the shoulder of another, and so on, until He came to the last one. He simply glanced at this woman and turned to go. 'Lord,' she said, 'why so little encouragement for me?' 'Because', He said, 'you, my daughter, at present must walk only by faith.'

God treats us in different ways at different times, but shows no favouritism (Romans 2:11); not one of His children fails to be within the scope of His constant goodness. We need to know ourselves and to give God all the glory when, in His kindness, He tempers and improves our strengths and encourages us to persevere in gaining the victory over our weaknesses. 'For from him and through him and for him are all things. To him be the glory for ever!' (Romans 11:36).

Accept one another, then, just as Christ accepted you,
in order to bring praise to God. (Romans 15:7)

## Food for thought

1. *Are you discontented with the circumstances of your life? How can you come to terms with your situation?*

2. *Why do we sometimes find ourselves in positions that exercise us so much?*

3. *Have you learned to distinguish between God's 'voice' and the devil's? What telltale signs help us to detect when it is the devil speaking?*

4. *Are you in danger of comparing yourself with others? Do you recognize that, as different parts of God's 'building', we complement one another?*

5. *Do you take into account that God deals with us in different ways at different periods of our lives? How should that change your attitude to your circumstances?*

**Notes**

1 Watson, 'An Extract from the Original Preface', Divine Cordial (first published 1663), p. 7.

2 From Charles Wesley's hymn 'Love Divine, All Loves Excelling'.

3 Grace is truly wonderful: since that time we have had more than thirty holidays with these lovely friends!

4 From George Wade Robinson's hymn 'Loved with Everlasting Love'.

# 18 Two great commands: obedience to Christ

*We demolish arguments and every pretension that sets itself up against the knowledge of God, and we take captive every thought to make it obedient to Christ. (2 Corinthians 10:5)*

*Love is not just a sentiment. Love is a great controlling passion and it always expresses itself in terms of obedience. (Martyn Lloyd-Jones)*

The greatest impetus to obedience is love. The more we love Christ, the more we will obey Him. If we are finding it difficult to obey, could it be that our love for the Saviour is not as it ought to be? For if we truly know Him and love Him, we will *desire* to obey, however difficult it may be; but if the desire is lacking, we are in an unhealthy condition.

If a group of people were working for a boss whom they never saw and who never communicated with them, they would become a very demoralized workforce: they might well lack pride in what they did. This can be true in society today: many people now work from home and are rarely in contact with the office base, so there is little face-to-face communication. Some who work in this way say that a lack of motivation can easily creep in.

The same can be true of us in a spiritual sense. The difference is that our 'boss' is in twenty-four-hour contact with us. But are we in contact with Him? Problems arise when we break our communication with Him: the longer we are out of contact, the less motivation we will have on the job.

## FORGET AND FORGO

With so many encouragements, so much support, so much consideration from the Master we serve, we should be the best servants in the world. We should be working as He wants us to, according to His 'memos', which we can only discover by reading His letters to us. 'And now . . . what does the LORD your God ask of you but to fear the LORD your God, to walk in obedience to him, to love him, to serve the LORD your God with all your heart and with all your soul' (Deuteronomy 10:12). But how easy it is to slip from this! How easily we can lose the drive and enthusiasm which we once had and the excitement which we once found in serving the Lord! Whereas we once hung upon the Lord's word and loved working for Him, we now sometimes stop listening and are more taken up with our own plans and schemes, forgetting and forgoing His will for our lives. And when this happens, we lose the joy and the sense of privilege in serving others.

## SERVE AND CARE

Although there are commands which are specific to particular roles people have—for example, commands to husbands and to wives, to parents and to children, to employers and to employees—there are also commands which apply to all believers, whatever our specific role and life calling. Supreme amongst these are the two great commands upon which, Jesus said, the entire law hangs: to love God and to love our neighbour. In His great 'upper room discourse' in John 13–16, Jesus taught, both verbally and by His example in washing His disciples' feet, that love for Him should be expressed in loving service of His people. While we are to love our neighbours as ourselves, Jesus made it very clear that a family bond exists amongst His disciples and this requires a specific love which each is to show for the other. Thus, on the great last day, the day of judgment, Christ's people will be identified as those who have served and cared for 'the least of [His] brothers and sisters' (Matthew 25:40). Paul makes a similar point when he tells the Galatian Christians that they are to do good to all people, especially to those of the household of faith (Galatians 6:10).

**TALK AND SHARE**

The importance of love for the Lord's people was beautifully illustrated in a wonderful incident in the life of the saintly Samuel Rutherford, the seventeenth-century Scottish pastor-preacher-theologian. One Saturday night an unknown visitor sought lodging at Rutherford's house. When catechizing the family that evening, Rutherford asked the stranger how many commandments there were, expecting the answer to be ten, and was surprised when the stranger replied, 'Eleven.' Rutherford believed the visitor to be in need of instruction, but the unusual guest insisted that there were eleven commandments, quoting Christ's words, 'A new command I give you: love one another' (John 13:34). Early the next morning, while Rutherford was meditating as he walked in a favourite spot, he was surprised to overhear a man praying beside a hedge. The man was pouring out his heart to God, asking Him to bless the people who would assemble that day in Rutherford's church! The Scottish pastor was profoundly moved and stirred by the man's prayer and realized that this was someone of unusual spirituality. It was the stranger to whom Rutherford had given hospitality the night before. All was revealed when the man introduced himself as James Ussher, Archbishop of Armagh and Primate of Ireland. He had come in disguise! Rutherford was a dyed-in-the-wool Presbyterian, and those were days when differences in one's church allegiance—Anglican or Presbyterian—mattered far more to Christians than is generally the case today; yet Christian love ran through Rutherford's and Ussher's spiritual veins. The two men talked and shared rich fellowship together, and, at Rutherford's request, Ussher preached that morning. The text? The new commandment!

### LOVE AND OBEY

If we all obeyed this command, we would be a united people, with united churches—something upon which God showers His blessing: 'How good and pleasant it is when God's people live together in unity! . . . For there the LORD bestows His blessing, even life for evermore' (Psalm 133:1, 3b). What blessing awaits us if we obey the following injunctions: 'A new command I give you: love one another. As I have loved you, so you must love one another' (John 13:34); 'If you love me, keep my commands . . . Whoever has my commands and keeps them is the one who loves me' (John 14:15, 21a); 'anyone who loves God must also love their brother and sister' (1 John 4:21b).

Love and obedience. Obeying Christ is the sure evidence of

the fact that we truly love Him. Evidence is something that can be *seen*. The arresting title of one of Francis Schaeffer's books is *The Church before the Watching World*. In another booklet, entitled *The Mark of the Christian*, Schaeffer wrote movingly of love and the visible unity to which it gives expression as the mark by which the world recognizes the Lord's people. This, of course, is what Jesus said: 'By this everyone will know that you are my disciples, if you love one another' (John 13:35). We need to remember that the world is watching, and it is to the people around us that we have been sent. They may not listen to our message, but they are certainly watching our lives. Loving our brothers and sisters is one of the greatest evidences of our love for the Master.

## THE POWER OF GOD

According to 1 Corinthians 13:7, love 'always trusts'. While we must never be naïve about human nature—even renewed, sanctified human nature—it is tragically possible for such biblical realism to degenerate into cynicism. 'He'll never change'; 'She'll never be any different.' How often we hear Christians speak like this of fellow believers! A highly respected preacher once said to my husband, 'Don't expect people to change after they are forty. Their characters are set by then.' My husband was shocked: it sounded to him as if the preacher did not believe that the gospel was the power of God unto salvation. This particular preacher had said this in response to my husband's question concerning a particularly distressing breakdown of relationship between one believer and his wife and another believer and his wife. He was at something of a loss to know the wisest way to deal with the problem. No doubt the older pastor-preacher was giving the benefit of years of experience of relationship breakdowns within church life. But to my husband, it sounded terribly cynical. And so it proved to be. Prayer was offered. And many years later, after the two couples had both moved to different areas and different churches, they eventually found themselves belonging to the same church again, though now in another town. But the old animosity had gone, and in place of coldness and distance there was now only warmth, mutual love and respect. The relationship breakdown had been particularly bad between the two wives. Yet the very last words of the wife as she lay dying were, 'How is . . . .?', and she uttered the name of the sister with whom the rift had once been so painfully acute. God's grace is truly wonderful, and true Christian love can conquer everything. 'Love covers over a multitude of sins' (1 Peter 4:8). God 'is able to do immeasurably more than all we ask or imagine, according to his power that is at work within us' (Ephesians 3:20).

**OVERLOOKING OFFENCES**

There are times, however, when we pray and do all that we can in a situation, but it does not produce such a blessed outcome. We need to remember that Scripture says, 'If it is possible, *as far as it depends on you*, live at peace with everyone' (Romans 12:18). We must do all we can to be reconciled to our brothers and sisters. In certain circumstances, of course, this may necessitate sharing matters with one or two others, and sometimes the church may need to get involved (Matthew 18:15–17). This is something of an extreme situation: we should not think, as some misguided believers have sometimes assumed, that every time someone ignores us or speaks hastily to us, we must exhort them and, if they do not agree with us, drag others into the situation: 'A person's wisdom yields patience; it is to one's glory to overlook an offence' (Proverbs 19:11). But there may be times when a situation is sufficiently serious for this to be the only God-honouring way to seek to resolve an issue. Should this be necessary, we are to leave the consequences with the Lord. Even then we must still remember that love 'always hopes' (1 Corinthians 13:7), and that it may be many years before we see the answers to our prayers.

### HIS CARE NEVER FALTERS

What blessings God confers upon us! What privileges we enjoy! What delight is ours in obeying, and how eager we should be to follow His commands! An expert in the law came to Jesus, testing Him with the question: 'Teacher, which is the greatest commandment in the Law?' The reply came in two all-embracing parts: '"Love the Lord your God with all your heart and with all your soul and with all your mind." This is the first and greatest commandment. And the second is like it: "Love your neighbour as yourself"' (Matthew 22:36–39). Through these two commands we get to know God better and love Him with greater ardour as we 'run the way of [His] commandments' (Psalm 119:32a, KJV). But as J. I. Packer reminds us,

What matters supremely . . . is not, in the last analysis, the fact that I know God, but the larger fact which underlines it—the fact that *he knows me*. I am graven on the palms of his hands. I am never out of his mind. All my knowledge of him depends on his sustained initiative in knowing me. I know him because he first knew me, and continues to know me. He knows me as a friend, one who loves me; and there is no moment when his eye is off me, or his attention distracted from me, and no moment, therefore, when his care falters.[1]

## Food for thought

1. *What is the greatest motivation for obedience?*

2. *Are you still listening to what God wants you to do? Do you ask Him to show you what you can do?*

3. *What are the two commands that should be paramount in our lives?*

4. *Can you think of instances in the Bible when God used dreams to speak to people? Has God spoken to you in this way?*[2]

**Notes**

[1] Packer, *Knowing God*, p. 41.

[2] A full discussion of dreams within the context of the completed canon of Scripture can be found in Archibald Alexander, 'Consideration on Dreams', ch. 7 of *Thoughts on Religious Experience* (Edinburgh: Banner of Truth Trust, 1967 (repr. 1978]), p. 79. Alexander was the first professor at Princeton Seminary. He was fully committed to the theology of the Westminster Standards. This makes his treatment of the subject all the more significant.

# Part 3. Value for sharing Him

# 19 Stretched horizons: the gospel

*As the rain and the snow*
   *come down from heaven,*
*and do not return to it*
   *without watering the earth*
*and making it bud and flourish . . .*
*So is my word that goes out from my mouth:*
   *it will not return to me empty,*
*but will accomplish what I desire*
   *and achieve the purpose for which I sent it. (Isaiah 55:10–11)*

*We should always look upon ourselves as God's servants, placed in God's world, to do his work; and accordingly labour faithfully for him; not with a design to grow rich and great, but to glorify God, and do all the good we possibly can. (David Brainerd)*

From time to time it is important that we stop where we are and halt what we are doing in order to ask ourselves why we are here and what the purpose of our lives is. I remember a conversation I had with a woman on the first occasion she came to our church. She had been thinking to herself that week, 'Surely there is more to life than having a happy family and a lovely home. Why am I here?' But do *our* horizons stretch further than our families, our homes and the immediacy of the things around us? If our lives just revolve around 'us and ours', we need to re-evaluate our fitness plan. We need to reassess the Lord's schedule for our lives, the work we have to do for *Him*. And that labour is meant to continue until we close our eyes on this world. Jesus left His disciples with the precise command to 'make disciples of all nations . . . teaching them to obey everything I have commanded you' (Matthew 28:19–20). They had become His followers, and now that He was leaving them they were to walk in His way: to reach out to others; to rescue people from their sin; and to go on to teach these people everything that He had taught them. In one sense, it was a very straightforward commission that He gave them, and that He has given to us. It is not at all complicated, but it can easily be *forgotten* when we take our eyes off the Saviour. It is not exactly obeying the command to 'deny [ourselves] and take up [our] cross daily and follow [Him]' (Luke 9:23b) if all our energies are being poured into our little lives and if we are living only for ourselves and our comforts. Of course, this does not mean that it is wrong to enjoy, even delight in, the good gifts which God has so freely and richly given us in this beautiful world that He has made; but it does mean that we should 'seek first his kingdom and his righteousness, and all these things will be given to you as well' (Matthew 6:33).

We have been told to go out into *all* the world and share the gospel—God alone can save! Then, when people are converted, we are told to teach them and show them *by example* how they should live to the glory of God. This is not just a commission for the pastors of our churches! We are to be like lights shining in this dark world; and we shall present very poor models if our goals are the same as those of the people around us. We are heading for glory, where our Saviour has already gone, and only then, when we have 'finished the race' (2 Timothy 4:7b), will we be able to

lay down our life's work of seeking the lost. Paul states in
1 Timothy 3:16, 'The mystery from which true godliness
springs is great: He appeared in the flesh . . . was preached
among the nations, was believed on in the world, was taken
up in glory.' That glory will dawn for us when our work on
earth is done.

We have this treasure from the Lord our God,
A gift of mercy from His hand;
His all-surpassing power at work in us,
To show His Glory and His plan.
For He has offered hope to all mankind,
Through sending Jesus to the cross;
And now this light He's shone into our hearts
We're holding out to all the world.[1]

We live in a vast, needy world. What do people need most
of all? Surely it is *the gospel* of our Lord Jesus Christ. But
how do we share this timeless gospel with the world, with the
people we interact with every day?

### AN INTERESTING NOTE

The problem is that people today have no thought of God
and scarcely spare Him a moment of their time. In former
generations, at times when the Spirit of God was very
evidently at work, people enquired after God, or at least
were present at Christian gatherings. We have been brought
into God's kingdom to be 'salt and light' to our generation.
How can we best serve the people we live amongst? Very
few, if any, will ask, 'How can I be saved?' or 'How can I
know my sins are forgiven?'[2] This means that we have to
think of the best and most effective ways to reach out to

lost humanity around us: the people on our doorsteps, our neighbours, work colleagues, and those with whom we brush shoulders every day. It is interesting to note how a number of Jesus' early disciples first found a brother or a friend and immediately shared with them that they had found the Messiah. For example, we read that 'the first thing Andrew did [after spending the day with Jesus] was to find his brother Simon and tell him, "We have found the Messiah" . . . And he brought him to Jesus' (John 1:41–42; see also v. 45). The disciples' exuberance and joy naturally overflowed to others around them.

### A HOLY CONCLAVE?

The best way we can be an influence for good with people is by being filled with the Holy Spirit. This is why it is so important to live in close communion with Christ, in obedience and love, and to know the life of His Spirit flooding our own. We are to *reach out*, and not live in a holy conclave where the only people we know and meet are in the church. And as we seek to reach those around us, we need constantly to pray for wisdom so that our lives will have an impact upon theirs.

We can often be so busy, in the church and for the church, that we have little time for people outside. I became aware of this a number of years ago. The only people I seemed to know, apart from my neighbours, were people in the church; so I began to pray that the Lord would bring me into contact with non-Christians. About that time we were having a family holiday. To enable our son to have company of his own age we suggested that he ask a friend along. As we were planning to holiday abroad we thought it best to introduce ourselves to his parents, just to show that we were 'normal'. (There was a debate at home about that!) We had a lovely evening with them, and by the end of the night our son's friend's mother had invited me along to the local group of the National Women's Register (NWR). This network was originally set up for professional women who move into an area, know very few people and wish to make friends. My local group met once a month and happened to be meeting the following week to discuss the topic 'The day that changed my life' (the following month's topic was 'A debt we could not pay'!). As you can imagine, I *knew* the Lord had opened this door in response to my prayer, and it provided very fruitful opportunities to share the gospel during the months I was able to attend. James 4:2 says, 'You do not have because you do not ask God.' This verse has often rebuked me. We are to ask the Lord to open doors. If the apostle Paul asked for prayer 'that God may open a door for our message, so that we may proclaim the mystery of Christ' (Colossians 4:3), we certainly need one another's prayers for these openings to occur for us.

### HIS, FROM BEGINNING TO END

When we are young Christians we often have 'zeal without wisdom'. I remember how, when I was first saved, I felt I had failed the Lord if I did not bring every conversation I had with unconverted people around to the gospel. I was frenetic! I could have been described as a 'head-hunter'. I may have had plenty of zeal, but I realize now that at times I certainly was not wise! Looking back, it is a wonder I had any friends who were non-believers: it is amazing they were not all frightened away. However, as we grow older, the danger is that we may have grown in our knowledge and wisdom but sadly declined in our zeal! It can be so thrilling when the Lord opens the door and surprises us with opportunities we have prayed for, and we acknowledge afresh that it is His work from beginning to end. What a privilege it is to work for God and with Him! Rebecca Manley Pippert speaks of being who we are, just where we are: 'Evangelism isn't just something you "do"— out there—and then get back to normal living. Evangelism involves taking people seriously . . . then sharing Christ as Lord in the context of our natural living situations . . . We, of all people, should be offering the world a picture of what it means to be truly human.'[3]

We can have a passion to reach the world, but we need to think strategically. Someone once wrote that if we have twelve bottles we wish to fill, we can either fill a bucket and throw it *at* the bottles (in which case, little will actually go in) or, to be more effective, we can get another bottle and from that fill each bottle individually. Henry Drummond speaks of a strategy that can be applied to 'soul-winning': 'Every atom in the universe can act upon every other atom, but only through the atom next to it. And if a man/woman would act upon every other man/woman, he can do so best by acting one at a time upon those beside him.'[4]

#### DRESSED . . . FOR THE LOST

We have been called upon by God to interact with the people who live next door or across the road, or whom we see at work, at the gym or in the shops. To relate to these people we need to be dressed in 'the beauty of holiness',[5] adorned with mercy and compassion, and filled with God's love for the lost. People may be attracted to what we have to say when they see Christ in us. The ideal personal evangelist is a Christian who every day is growing in likeness to Jesus. How Christ loved people—even enough to die for them! What a high calling we have! We can only reflect our Saviour as we seek day by day to walk in step with Him. 'For the Spirit God gave us does not make us timid, but gives us power, love and self-discipline. So do not be ashamed of the testimony about our Lord' (2 Timothy 1:7–8). God communicates with us, and it is our responsibility to share Him with those with whom we have contact. There are so many needy people in our world: there is plenty of scope, as long as we are looking around us and not being preoccupied with ourselves. Sharing our lives with others is displaying Christ's love and following His example.

**NOT AN OPTION—A COMPULSION**

Have we a desire to make our Saviour known? If not, why not? If this is the work we have been called to do, it is not an option for more zealous souls. Are we waiting around for others who we feel are more capable of getting on with the work? Are we prepared to stand by and watch and even pray for them, but not ever to think of being part of the 'team'? Our lack of personal action can sometimes be the result of an absence of conviction and concern that every impenitent soul is *utterly lost*. Someone once said, 'No man can be a herald of His Lord's passion if he does not himself share it.'

If we saw people dropping down dead around us for want of some antidote that would save their lives, there would be something wrong if we could pass by unconcerned on the other side. A sick soul needs a prescription, not a lecture about different types of medicine. There is only one prescription we have to offer for this illness: Christ's blood; and it can heal any sin-saturated soul. The Lord Jesus Christ is the remedy for every disease of the soul: He can heal the worst complaint. We *know* people are perishing (do we?), but we need to *feel* it, and we need to ask God to give us that compulsion that will activate us to be soul-winners in His service; to think of others, not just to think of our own ease. People are blindly falling over a spiritual precipice to their deaths: we need to take them by the hand and direct them from the cliff-edge to Mount Calvary. Spurgeon, the great evangelist, said,

Even if I were utterly selfish, and had no care for anything but my own happiness, I would choose, if I might, under God, to be a soul-winner; for never did I know perfect, overflowing, unutterable happiness of the purest and most ennobling order, till I first heard of one who had sought and found the Saviour through my means. No young mother ever so rejoiced over her first-born child, no warrior was so exultant over a hard-won victory.[6]

**WE ARE WATCHED**

God can use us just where we are, whatever we are doing, and in His own way. We need to be alert to every opportunity of speaking for Him. But there are times when it is not speech that challenges the unbeliever, but things we do—or do not do! The world is not short-sighted when it comes to viewing the Christian, more often than not in a condemnatory manner. When I first began teaching, another woman started teaching at the same school on the same day as I did. On one occasion we were the only two in the staff room, where we had arrived early for lunch. As we were talking she suddenly broke into the conversation to say, 'I caught you!' I wondered what I had done, but she quickly went on to tell me: 'You never gave thanks for your food!' My usual practice at lunchtime was to offer a silent prayer of thanks for my food. Usually I must have closed my eyes, and unbeknown to me, this colleague had been watching me. On the day in question I had silently thanked the Lord for my food but had not closed my eyes. My colleague was delighted to tell me that she had 'caught me out'! I told her that as I was only eating an apple for lunch, and as we had been talking, I had given thanks to God with my eyes open. But that conversation remained a lasting reminder to me that the world notices every move we make as Christians and is always ready to help us with the creases we may have in our clothing. Spurgeon again gives good advice:

My brethren, let me say, be like Christ at all times. Imitate him . . . We are watched; our words are caught; our lives are examined . . . Let us live the life of Christ . . . Let us take care that we exhibit our Master, and not ourselves—so that we can say, 'It is no longer I who lives, but Christ who lives in me.'[7]

### A FAILED DIET!

I recall another occasion, this time when I was a student, when 'actions spoke louder than words'. I and another friend spent hours of our time with a student who had many questions about the Christian faith. We felt we were getting nowhere with her. Then, just before Christmas, my friend wanted to lose a couple of kilos before going home and asked if I would help by joining her in the endeavour. Looking back, I see it was ludicrous. She really *did* need to lose weight, but I was like a whippet: not a gram of fat on me! However, to help her with her diet, I agreed to join her. We ate a boiled egg for breakfast, lunch and dinner. After a few days I was beginning to feel rather weak: a few times a day we had to climb at least eighty steps to our rooms, and three eggs were not enough fuel to keep me on my feet! The diet lasted until the third day, when it was abruptly brought to a halt by the enticing aroma of *sausage and chips* issuing from the refectory. That broke the spell for me—and for my friend.

When we returned after the Christmas holidays we were thrilled to hear of the conversion of the girl we had spent so many hours with during the previous term. When we enquired as to what had brought her to faith, she cited our failed diet! However could such a failure have brought someone to salvation? Her reasoning was this: she had watched us very carefully to see if what we said matched the way we lived. When she witnessed how weak our self-discipline was with regard to the diet, she concluded that our ability to stay consistent in our behaviour as Christians was sustained by Someone outside of ourselves. The only answer that satisfied her was God! How glad we were about that failed diet! God can use the most amazing means to bring people to Himself.

### STEP OUT OF OUR BOATS

There is no let-out clause for the person who has joined the family of God. We have a work to do: we were saved, not simply to sit around and to indulge ourselves, but to serve

(Hebrews 9:14b). We have been given a job and have at our disposal all the resources we need to complete it. So it is pointless saying, 'I'm hopeless at witnessing, I just can't do it.' That surely is like saying, 'I'm alive, but I can't breathe'! We are to be ourselves just where we are, loving people and 'dying' to see them saved. Witnessing for Christ and seeking to win others for Him is not a gift; it is our calling, our responsibility. We are called to confess Christ, and we have been bought by Him so as to go into the marketplace to speak for Him. That is what God expects of every one of His children: He has no 'secret' disciples. He who calls us will surely supply all the necessary power and ability to perform. We are to step out of our boats in faith (Matthew 14:22–33).

Neither do people light a lamp and put it under a bowl. Instead they put it on its stand, and it gives light to everyone in the house. In the same way, let your light shine before others, that they may see your good deeds and glorify your Father in heaven. (Matthew 5:15–16)

## Food for thought

1. *What does the world desperately need?*
2. *What is the scope of your work for God? Does it tend to concentrate on your family and friends alone? Does it include unbelievers?*
3. *Do you have any non-Christian friends? If not, are you concerned that you are not reaching those 'in the world'?*
4. *In relation to our witness, how important are the things we do compared with our words?*

**HIS TREASURED POSSESSION**

**Notes**

1 Mike Busbee, Lou Fellingham and Nathan Fellingham, 'Treasure'.

2 See Appendix 9, 'The Room'.

3 Manley Pippert, *Out of the Saltshaker*, p. 30.

4 Drummond, *New Evangelism*, pp. 258–259.

5 From John Samuel Bewley Monsell's hymn, 'O Worship the Lord in the Beauty of Holiness'; and Robin Mark, 'In the Beauty of Holiness'.

6 Spurgeon, *Soul Winner* (1905), p. 249.

7 C. H. Spurgeon, '21. Christ's People: Imitators of Him', Answers in Genesis, https://answersingenesis.org/education/spurgeon-sermons/21-christs-people-imitators-of-him/.

# 20 True and authentic: love, love, and more love

*This is how God showed his love among us: he sent his one and only Son into the world that we might live through him. This is love: not that we loved God, but that he loved us and sent his Son as an atoning sacrifice for our sins. (1 John 4:9–10)*

*Take the fact that you were created to love. Your heart can find real joy only through love—through loving and being loved. (Thomas Goodwin)*

Spurgeon once asked, 'Do you have a love for the lost in your heart? If you don't, you are probably one of them!' But in our busy lives we can lose the plot; or we can be so busy *in* the work that we forget that the most important things in life are not *things* but *people*. How are we meant to reach the mass of people all around us? The answer is, 'We won't!' As we saw in the last chapter, God wants us to befriend those whom He has placed on our doorstep. God's Word tells us that we in our small corners 'are God's handiwork, created in Christ Jesus to do good works, which God prepared in advance for us to do' (Ephesians 2:10). God has given each one of us specific work to do for Him that only we can do. Each of us has a unique job description! Yes, the 'world' that orbits around *us* needs to see *love*, *love*, and more *love*. It sees very little of the true authentic article in the world of movies, pop stars, television, and the like, so we are called upon to show it through the way we live and interact with others.

In the effort to convey the magnitude of God's love in Christ for this fallen world, the following graphic story has often been told:

There was a man who worked at a country railway station during the days when signals had to be changed by hand. There was some intricate machinery between the levers in the signal box and the points on the track, which enabled the points to move when the levers were pulled. The man had a son who was still only a toddler, and he had taken the lad to the signal box for an hour. A train was due along the stretch of track and this necessitated moving the points. Just as the man was about to move them, he noticed that his son had fallen into the part of the machinery where the various cogs would turn as the levers were pulled. Not to pull them would mean that the train, with many passengers on board, would plough into a stationary train on the other track. But if the man were to pull the levers, his son would be ground between the various cogs and would inevitably be crushed to death. The choice was agonizing, but the man knew that he could not allow the train to crash, thereby killing and injuring the many passengers on board. So he pulled the levers, the points moved, and the train passed by in safety, the passengers, with their smiling faces, utterly ignorant of these events. As the train passed, the man cried out, 'You just don't understand, you just don't understand, you will never know the cost!'

Sadly, this story seriously distorts the Bible's teaching concerning the love of God which is displayed supremely in the death of the Lord Jesus Christ. The story may well illustrate the cost to the father—and to his son—of ensuring that the passengers were 'saved' through the father's 'sacrificing' of his son. And yet it is a very poor and dangerous illustration of the love of God in delivering up his Son to the death of the cross to save sinful human beings.

To begin with, the passengers were entitled to travel safely on the train. Next, it was surely rather foolhardy of the father to take his son where he would be exposed to such danger: how could the father do his job properly and take appropriate care of his son? Again, the father was probably motivated by the fact that it would have been wrong *in those circumstances of his own making* to allow the passengers to die to save his son. And, lastly, the son was oblivious to what was happening.

## VAST BEYOND ALL MEASURE

Now consider what took place at the cross. We had forfeited all claims and 'rights' upon God. We were justly and rightly subject to his condemnation. Our dangerous position was that for which we, not God, were responsible. But moved by undeserved love for us, the Father, the Son and the Holy Spirit agreed that the Father would send the Son, the Son would come willingly, and the Holy Spirit would support and sustain the Son in the great work of procuring salvation for His people. It was not only the Father who demonstrated His love towards us in the delivering up of His Son to the death of the cross; the Son also, as Paul expressed it, 'loved me and gave himself for me' (Galatians 2:20). And Paul also writes of 'the love of the Spirit' (Romans 15:30b). How much greater is this—the united love and work of the Father, the Son and the Holy Spirit for the salvation of undeserving rebels—than what the man in the signal box did! And it is this love—this amazing love of the three-in-one God, and at *such cost*—that we have to tell of to those living around us: the story of a Saviour's blood and agonizing death, bearing the awful weight of human sin and of divine wrath upon that sin; the magnitude of the love of the Father in delivering up His one and only, dearly beloved Son for us; and the love of the Spirit in sustaining the Son through those terrible hours of darkness, and then in bringing to our ruined lives the salvation which the Son has procured for us:

How deep the Father's love for us,
How vast beyond all measure,
That He should give His only Son
To make a wretch *His treasure*.
How great the pain of searing loss—
The Father turns His face away,
As wounds which mar the Chosen One
Bring many sons to glory.[1]

### DISTINCTIVE AND SACRIFICIAL

When we know *that* love, we will view the world very differently. If Christ did all that for us, there is nothing we should not be prepared to do for Him and for others. 'To him who loves us and has freed us from our sins by his blood, and has made us to be a kingdom and priests to serve his God and Father—to him be glory and power for ever and ever!' (Revelation 1:5b–6). We are in a very bad way spiritually if we never consider that God wants us to pass on the message of His great love to those who are around us. Nicky Gumbel writes of a young police officer who in his final exam was given one of the following questions:

### HIS TREASURED POSSESSION

'You are on patrol in outer London when an explosion occurs in a gas main in a nearby street. On investigation you find that a large hole has been blown in the footpath and there is an overturned van lying nearby. Inside the van there is a strong smell of alcohol. Both occupants—a man and a woman—are injured. You recognise the woman as the wife of your Divisional Inspector, who is at present away in the USA. A passing motorist stops to offer you assistance and you realise he is a man who is wanted for armed robbery. Suddenly a man runs out of a nearby house, shouting that his wife is expecting a baby and that the shock of the explosion has made the birth imminent. Another man is crying for help, having been blown into an adjacent canal by the explosion, and he cannot swim.

'Bearing in mind the provisions of the Mental Health Act, describe in a few words what actions you would take.'

The officer thought for a moment, picked up his pen, and wrote: 'I would take off my uniform and mingle with the crowd.'

We can sympathise with the answer. As a Christian, it is often easier to take off our Christian uniform and 'mingle with the crowd'. But we are called to remain distinctive, to retain our Christian identity, wherever we are and whatever the circumstances.[2]

A supreme example of someone who remained distinctive was Jim Elliot, who, together with a number of other young Christian missionaries, was martyred when he took the gospel to the Auca Indians. He had once written the words, 'He is no fool who gives what he cannot keep to gain what he cannot lose.' The world needs to *see* God's love in us: genuine, distinctive, *sacrificial* love. Ephesians 5:1–2 encourages us to 'follow God's example . . . as dearly loved children and live a life of love, just as Christ loved us and gave himself up for us as a fragrant offering and sacrifice to God.' A watching world will see it and take note.

### OUT ON A LIMB

There is a very moving account of personal love and sacrifice in *The Secret Thoughts of an Unlikely Convert* by Rosaria Champagne Butterfield. She is a converted university professor who was previously in a lesbian relationship. She was wonderfully converted through the witness, friendship and love of a minister and his wife who had welcomed her into their home and who had simply got to know her. Over a two-year period their *lives* spoke to her. Not long after her conversion she was faced with a challenge: one of her students had tried to commit suicide by setting fire to herself, and when Rosaria visited her at the hospital, she knew that this was 'God's work for me, right now'. What a challenge! But Rosaria rose to it and for a time invited the student to live at home with her.[3] There were many other similar situations awaiting her. We too may be faced with challenges when we have to be willing to sacrifice our personal comforts and plans. But we need to keep our eyes open and be able to see where the Lord may be calling us to 'go out on a limb' for Him in serving others, as Rosaria did. Did not Jesus Himself say, 'I am among you as one who serves' (Luke 22:27b)? What this means is that there will be some situations which present themselves which obviously require us to respond by serving others as part of our service of the Lord; but there will be other times when things will not be so self-evident, and yet, if we are watchful, alert and enterprising, we will both see and seize the opportunity to 'do good to all people, especially to those who belong to the family of believers' (Galatians 6:10).

## KEEP OUR EYES OPEN

Examples abound in the Bible of those who saw opportunities to do good and who made the most of them. The supreme example is, of course, our Lord Jesus Christ, who 'went around doing good' (Acts 10:38). Even when He was dying a terrible death on the cross, He made provision for a home for His mother (John 19:25–27). Or we could think of the woman who anointed Jesus with the precious perfume in anticipation of His burial (John 12:3 8), or of Paul helping to collect brushwood to build a fire for his fellow shipwrecked prisoners and passengers in Malta (Acts 28:3–6). We may not be presented with such dramatic opportunities, but we can be just as helpful in our service if we only keep our eyes open to the needs which are around us. Some of us may be in a position to open our homes, just as the minister and his wife did when they befriended Rosaria. It is important that we love people, and that they know that we love them and want to be true friends with them, rather than some kind of 'head-hunters'. We surely need to avoid being like those of whom C. S. Lewis once spoke, who were always seeking to 'help others'. One could tell who 'the others' were, Lewis caustically observed, by the worried, hunted look upon their faces!

## THE LONG HAUL

These days there is a tendency to think only of ourselves, our families, and, if we have the time, our friends. Jesus had very different ideas, ideas which He shared with a prominent Pharisee and his friends. He told them that they should invite those who could not repay them, and he then went on tell the parable of the great banquet. How often do we think of 'the poor, the crippled, the blind and the lame' (Luke 14:21b), those who cannot return the favour? To entertain only family or friends has become such a well-established practice, even amongst Christians, that there is a danger that little contact will be made with those outside the church. But the heart of God is seen in Jesus' parable: He says, 'Compel them to come in' (14:23). Effort is needed on our part if we intend to engage with people on the 'roads and country lanes' of our towns and cities.

We meet people in the highways and byways, but more often than not, at work. There is often limited time and opportunity over lunch or a morning break—where such things still exist in our high-pressured world!—to interact with those with whom we are employed. In the world of work there is little opportunity to get to know people really well. So why not invite them into our homes? We need more than a fleeting contact with people in order to speak about the most precious treasure in our lives, and that subject may not surface until some way down the road. We have to be prepared for the long haul: friendships have to be forged and trust built up.

## OUR HEARTS AND HOMES

If we have busy lifestyles it can be quite sacrificial, time-wise, to invite people round, especially if both the husband and wife are working. Younger people or young couples may prefer to meet up with others for sport. But to really get to know people will require more than just doing sport together: it is in the socializing afterwards that relationships are most likely to be forged. But in the busy modern world, it may well be that socializing afterwards is what people will not have time for. So where do we go from there? Jesus spent much of his time speaking and teaching when sharing a meal with others. Is He not our great example? We too may be able to have meaningful conversations with neighbours, work colleagues and others over a meal.

If we invite people for a meal, we need to keep a few things in mind. First—especially if you feel a bit daunted at having people for a meal—it needs to be said that the meal does not need to be anything impressive: we are not seeking to show off our culinary abilities but, rather, are opening our hearts and homes to others. In these days of *Ready, Steady, Cook* programmes and books like *Beyond Beans on Toast*, there are plenty of ideas around for simple but nutritious and delicious meals which will not take a day and a half to prepare.[4] We need to focus on making people feel welcome and at home. We need to give thought to *the time* at which we want them to arrive and *the time* at which we plan to eat.

I recall an occasion when my husband and I invited two couples—two Christian women we knew, with their unbelieving husbands—along for an evening meal. Having only just begun to tuck in, we heard a knock on the dining-room door and in trooped our children (who had already eaten!), looking very forlorn and woebegone, holding their tummies and saying that they were starving! Though amusing, it was obviously embarrassing for our visitors. We certainly could have done without the distraction of one of us having to leave the table to take the children back to bed! If at all possible, then, it is better to choose a time when it *might* just be that the children are sleeping or at least settled. This is one of a number of aspects to be considered, especially if hospitality is being used as a means of getting to know people, with a possibility of sharing our faith.

## DO WHAT YOU CAN

Some may say that they are not conversationalists, that they are too quiet to have people into their homes, and would certainly find it difficult to give them a meal. But have you ever tried? I remember a dear elderly unmarried Christian lady who was very quiet and who found it difficult to make conversation. Furthermore, her first language—the language of 'heart and home'—was Welsh, and she was living in a part of Wales which was predominantly English-speaking. She could well have thought that she was unable to open her home to others. But, like the woman who anointed Jesus, 'she did what she could' (Mark 14:8). On Sundays she regularly invited to her flat for a meal two young women in their early twenties who occasionally attended the church to which she belonged. One young woman was from a Christian home and had a Christian background. The other was very different and would probably be called 'a party girl'. Although so different from this elderly believer in age, interests and a hundred and one other things, the two younger women obviously enjoyed sharing her home for a couple of hours and quite probably provided the conversation. One of the women eventually came to faith in Christ. This dear elderly lady was a wonderful witness to the grace of God. She did what she could! How important it is to do what we can, rather than bemoan our inability to do what we cannot!

## A DEMONSTRATION

As the writer to the Hebrews puts it, 'I do not have time . . . ' (Hebrews 11:32) to enumerate the many reasons for being hospitable as a means of demonstrating true Christian love for those about us.[5] Suffice it to say that one of the strongest arguments for showing hospitality is that we are *commanded* to do so, opening our hearts and homes to others, whether they are believers or not. This having been said, the command to show hospitality must be understood in a sensible way. Someone with an unconverted spouse may well be unable to do this. Equally, there may be other domestic demands which make it impossible to show hospitality. After all, if we are to invite those who cannot repay the offer of hospitality, it follows that there must be some people who cannot offer it. When Jesus said that the Son of Man had nowhere to lay His head (Matthew 8:20), He was in a position where He was unable to open up an earthly home of His own to give hospitality. Furthermore, just as we saw that there is a spiritual gift of faith which is different from the gift of saving faith which the Lord gives to all His people, so too there is a special gift of serving: 'If your gift is serving, devote yourself to serving others' (Romans 12:7, ISV). And one example of serving is to provide hospitality. It is undoubtedly the case that some believers, either as a result of the temperament with which God has blessed them and/or as a result of their life circumstances, are far better placed to provide hospitality

**HIS TREASURED POSSESSION**

on a regular basis than are other believers. We need to discern whether this is something for which the Lord has especially gifted us.

## LIFELESS AND LOVELESS

Let us now move on to consider opening our homes, not as a means of getting to know those who are not believers, but as a means of fellowship with the saints. The church lives out her life before a watching world. And the world watches not only how we relate to it, but also how we relate to our Christian brothers and sisters. What does it see? Consider the following real-life example I once heard: a church had invited a man to preach one Sunday but sent him to a cafe for his lunch! No welcoming home where he would be provided with a meal to share with one or more from the church! No place to rest in the afternoon between the morning and the evening meetings! One could hardly imagine the world behaving like this. They would at least have sent him to a restaurant, not a cafe! What would the unbelieving world think of such a church 'family'? Alexander Strauch, in his book *The Hospitality Command*, introduces us to several inhospitable churches and Christians.[6] One can only conclude that the churches to which those cited in his book went had not read certain parts of the Bible. The Word of God is full of commands to 'show hospitality'.[7] Strauch tells of a single woman who attended his church and related to him the following experience that dramatically illustrates why we need fresh teaching on this subject:

At one time in her life, she had travelled more than an hour by bus every Sunday to attend a small suburban Church. Each week after the Sunday morning service, she would eat alone in a restaurant and then spend the entire afternoon in a park or library so that she could attend the evening service. She did this for four years. What left her with sour memories of this church was the fact that in four years no-one invited her home to eat a Sunday afternoon meal or to rest. It wasn't until she announced she was leaving that an elderly woman in the church invited her home for a meal on her final Sunday.[8]

This is but one example of lifeless, loveless, inhospitable Christians who through their thoughtlessness can bring much heartache to fellow believers and give an inexcusably poor witness to the world. A cold, unfriendly, unloving church contradicts the gospel message. Hospitality is something we need to see revived; it bespeaks Christian virtue.

### PULLING UP THE DRAWBRIDGE

But there might be some who would question or even object to this way of displaying Christian love? They might ask, 'Should everyone be involved in hospitality?' Allowing for the kinds of exceptions we have already noted and a number of others, the answer is a resounding 'yes'.[9] But many, sadly, have never known the blessing such giving can bring. Why might this be? Alexander Strauch suggests some challenging possibilities as to why we fail to do what God commands:

At heart we are selfish, and selfishness is the single greatest enemy of hospitality. We do not want to be inconvenienced. We do not want to share our privacy or time with others. We are consumed with our personal comforts. We want to be free to go about our business without interference or concern for other people's needs. We don't want the responsibility and work that hospitality entails. We are greedy and don't want to share our food, home, or money. We are afraid that we will be used or that our property will sustain damage.[10]

In her book *A Cup of Cold Water* Julia Jones speaks of an all too common reason for not showing hospitality: 'Many of us are guilty of pulling up the drawbridge to protect our space. We feel that to invite strangers in is an invasion of our privacy. We can't imagine feeling comfortable with those whom we don't already know well.'[11]

## 'UTTER RUBBISH'

The late John Thomas points out another problem which prevents some from knowing the privileges and blessings of serving God in this way. He states in one of his sermons in *Contender for the Faith*,

I am sometimes grieved that we deprive ourselves of blessings because we do not use our homes as we ought. The blessings that I have received in my home through entertainment [hospitality] are far greater than any I have given. I commend it to you to exercise hospitality. If you have a home, never mind how plain it is . . . use it, and you will find that the blessing of God will be upon you . . . The blessing of God is upon the entertainer and the entertained. May God give us grace to use our homes! People ask me sometimes, 'What can I do for God?' My friend, is there anybody here who cannot do this? Do not dare to say that your home is not good enough! That before God is utter rubbish . . . God is not concerned about the quality of your carpets or your china or anything else: what He is concerned about is your open heart and your open door, and His blessing will be upon it.[12]

## HINGES AND A LOCK

All of these attitudes are selfish, and selfishness is sin.

HIS TREASURED POSSESSION

Thinking only of oneself is a mark of the old unregenerate life. It is worldliness; it is the opposite of love; and it is quite contrary to the 'law' of hospitality. It is totally opposed to everything Jesus Christ taught and lived. He is our example: He lived his life for others. Therefore, we must confess our sinful selfishness towards God and His people. We must seek to serve one another gladly as He served us, and thereby partake of the love He intends His people to share with one another and with the world.

In so doing, however, we must not fall into another extreme. If we are married and/or have children, we must not neglect our spouses and families. We may have parents or siblings who live with us, and we are to be sensitive to their needs. Again, we must get the right balance in this area of Christian living. Some have their doors open all the time; others never open them. Some do not know how to spend time with their families but always have people coming and going; others can never see past their own family units. There is an insightful comment in Edith Schaeffer's book *What Is a Family?*: 'A family is a door that has hinges and a lock. The hinges should be well oiled to swing the door open during certain times, but the lock should be firm enough to let people know that the family needs to be alone part of the time, just to be a family.'[13]

How we need to demonstrate the right balance in the expressions of love we show before the world! May we see many in glory who will be able to say that they came to love God through seeing His love mirrored in us.

Love must be sincere. Hate what is evil; cling to what is good.

Be devoted to one another in love. Honour one another above yourselves. Never be lacking in zeal, but keep your spiritual fervour, serving the Lord . . . Share with the Lord's people who are in need. Practise hospitality. (Romans 12:9–11, 13)

## Food for thought

1. *Do you daily remember God's great love for you? Do you have a love for the lost?*

2. *Do you know anything of sacrificial love? Can you think of times when you have been sacrificial in demonstrating your love towards others?*

3. *Should everyone be involved in hospitality? Can you think of reasons why you should offer hospitality?*

4. *Who are the people you should be inviting to share hospitality?*

5. *What things may cause people to feel they cannot offer hospitality? Are there times when we should refuse to offer hospitality?*

6. *In what ways can we be thoughtful in practising hospitality? List the benefits we receive if we regularly practise hospitality.*

7. *How important is it sometimes to have a 'closed' door?*

### Notes

1  Stuart Townend, 'How Deep the Father's Love for Us'; emphasis added.

2  Gumbel, *Question of Life*, pp. 234–235. The book from which this quote is taken has some excellent material in it but also contains some things relating to the nature of the church and to spiritual gifts which I consider to be unscriptural and harmful. For this reason, I am quoting from this book but am not thereby recommending it.

**HIS TREASURED POSSESSION**

**3** Butterfield, *Secret Thoughts of an Unlikely Convert*, p. 61.

**4** See Appendix 10, 'A Mix and Match Recipe'.

**5** There are many questions on the whole subject of hospitality. See Appendix 11, 'Discussion Questions on Hospitality'.

**6** Strauch, *Hospitality Commands*, p. 5.

**7** See Appendix 12, 'Bible Verses on Hospitality'.

**8** Strauch, *Hospitality Commands*, p. 5. See also Appendix 13, 'Extract from Alexander Strauch, The Hospitality Commands'.

**9** See Appendix 12 'Bible Verses on Hospitality'.

**10** Strauch, *Hospitality Commands*, p. 38.

**11** Jones, *Cup of Cold Water*, p. 11.

**12** Thomas, *Contender for the Faith*, p. 23. *Contender for the Faith* was not produced by John Thomas but published posthumously, using tapes of some of his sermons.

**13** Schaeffer, *What Is a Family?*, p. 211.

# 21 Never stop: prayer, prayer, and more prayer

*Be alert and of sober mind so that you may pray. (1 Peter 4:7b)*

*Talking to men for God is a great thing, but talking to God for men is greater still. He will never talk well and with real success to men for God who has not learned well how to talk to God for men. (E. M. Bounds)*

Who is going to pray for our families, our non-Christian friends and our neighbours? In one sense it is true to say that if we do not do so, nobody will. If people have no Christian family, friends, colleagues and acquaintances, then, apart from Christians' general prayers for a lost world, there will be nobody who will specifically pray for them. This leaves us with a great responsibility, and we have to ask ourselves if we have realized the weight of this responsibility and have risen to the challenge which it brings. Have we prayed unceasingly through the years for that husband, wife, child, relative, friend, work colleague or neighbour, even for those whom we might regard as enemies?

Wales is a small country; some of its Christian leaders may be known elsewhere in the UK but, generally speaking, those whose lives will be seen to have spoken for eternity remain largely unknown (the towering figure of the late Dr Martyn Lloyd-Jones is a key exception, as his spiritual impact extended across Europe, Africa and America when he was alive, and extends even further afield today through the publication of his sermons in books and on the Internet). This is, perhaps, unfortunate because some of Wales's leaders were evidently men whose prayers were 'powerful and effective' (James 5:16b). A striking example of persevering and prevailing prayer was provided by the late Elwyn Davies, General Secretary of the Evangelical Movement of Wales, in a tribute which he wrote on the death of a man named Idris Williams, who was the father-in-law of the late Hugh Morgan, a pastor-preacher who was greatly used in Wales and throughout the UK. Idris Williams had become a Christian through the consistent and steadfast prayers of a work colleague. Something of the prayer which lay behind his conversion and which God used to bring him to faith was related in Elwyn Davies' tribute:

Mr Williams came to the Lord Jesus Christ as a young man . . . A story associated with his conversion bears repeating. Immediately after his conversion he went to the works smithy to tell a godly man by the name of William Bell that he had found the Lord. William Bell did something which took Mr Williams completely by surprise. He walked to the wall of the smithy and took a nail out of a piece of wood. 'That's Idris Williams!' he said, holding up the nail. There were a number of nails in that piece of wood, and each represented a person for whose salvation William Bell had been praying.[1]

This, however, was not the end of the story of the effectiveness of intercessory prayer in the life of Idris Williams. Partly as a result of the widespread liberal influences in many of the churches in Wales in the mid-twentieth century, Idris began to drift spiritually and lost his way. His son-in-law and daughter gave themselves to earnest prayer for him, and the spiritual breakthrough came: Idris Williams knew spiritual restoration and a renewed walk with the Lord.[2] The importance of being earnest—certainly in the realm of prayer!

### IMPORTUNITY AND URGENCY

We have scriptural warrant to believe that God will hear our fervent prayers: 'The prayer of a righteous person is powerful and effective' (James 5:16b). C. H. Spurgeon knew all about this kind of praying: importunity and urgency characterized his prayers. He loved people—sinful people—and was 'dying' for them to be saved:

I do not see how our sense of oneness to Christ could ever have been perfected if we had not been permitted to work for Him. If He had been pleased to save us by His precious blood, and then leave us with nothing to do, we would have had fellowship with Christ up to a certain point, but (I speak from experience) there is no fellowship with Christ that seems so vivid, so real to the soul, as when we try to win a soul for Him. Oh, when I come to battle with that soul's difficulties, to weep over that soul's hardness . . . when I am in an agony of spirit, and feel that I could die sooner than that soul perish, then I get to read the heart of Him whose flowing tears . . . and dying wounds showed how much He loved poor fallen mankind.[3]

Surely such concern for people will find expression in intercessory prayer for them. If the Saviour was willing to *die* for people, surely we should not find it too difficult a matter to *pray* for them. My husband and I have been in contact for nearly forty years with a certain man who had the privilege of being brought up in an evangelical church but who, over the years, has shown little interest in Christian things. A few years ago I offered him a book by Peter Jeffery entitled *I Will Never Become A Christian*. I was pleased that he accepted it from me and said that he would read it. A very surprising conversation ensued, all the more so because this man is a particularly private individual. He shared with me that during the previous week he had been thinking that his whole life was utterly fruitless and futile. He said that he 'envied' my husband and me because 'you have it all right down here, and all right up there'. We do not know what God is doing in the hearts of people in response to our prayers. We are to pray, and then leave the underground work to Him.

**GOD USES THE TRUTH**

Many could share similar experiences. The lesson is not to give up. God sometimes gives us these little encouragements and 'snapshots' into His dealings with people in order to keep us praying, 'but blessed are those who have not seen and yet have believed' (John 20:29b). In the area of intercessory prayer this means that in some situations we shall never see the results of our prayers on earth.

One of the most striking illustrations of this truth is seen in the ministry of a great Puritan preacher, John Flavel. On one occasion Flavel preached on the verse 'If anyone does not love the Lord, let that person be cursed!' (1 Corinthians 16:22). Present in the congregation was a fifteen-year-old lad named Luke Short. He subsequently emigrated to New England, where he worked as a farmer and lived to a great age. One day, in his hundredth year,

as he sat in his fields reflecting upon his long life, he recalled
a sermon he had heard in Dartmouth as a boy before he
sailed to America. The horror of dying under the curse of
God was impressed upon him as he meditated on the words
he had heard so long ago and he was converted to Christ—
eighty-five years after hearing John Flavel preach.[4]

While it is clear that Short remembered both the matter of
the sermon and the manner of Flavel's preaching it—as well
as the effect of it upon the people—more was obviously at
work in his conversion than these things: otherwise, he would
have been converted the day he heard the message. What
happened when he was 100 years old was that God brought
the truth powerfully to bear upon him and renewed his heart
so that he embraced the gospel. But if God used the truth thus
remembered to bring him to faith, surely this was also an
answer to the prayer which Flavel would have prayed in the
meeting at which he preached this message: that God would
bless the truth to the salvation of the hearers.[5] As was the case
with Daniel, Flavel's prayer was heard and answered, but
a period of time elapsed before the evidence of that answer
became apparent (see Daniel 10:12–14). We are to pray and
to leave the consequences with God. Eternity will tell!

### IN NEED OF A BATH

Sometimes God will, in His kindness and mercy, show us the
beginning and the end of our prayers. When I was a student,
I returned home for the holidays on one occasion to discover
that a man was carrying out some decorating work at my
parents' house. I fell into conversation with him, and he soon
told me that he was a communist and that his grandmother

was a spiritualist. I shared the glorious gospel with him to the best of my ability. Within a day or two he had finished the work and left. In the ensuing years he would often come to mind when I was praying, so I regularly prayed for him. I completed my course as a student, began working, and then married and moved to another area. About six years after meeting the decorator, I was visiting my parents one Easter and went to what had been my home church for a Good Friday meeting. To my surprise, there was the decorator entering the church, carrying a Bible under his arm! Although the Good Friday meeting was a glorious occasion, I was almost impatient for it to end so that I might speak with the man. To my joy and delight I discovered that he had been converted! But even more thrilling was the fact that his wife was with him, and she had also been converted. He told me that after finishing the work in my home he had started work in a house on the other side of the town, where he had met a young man who shared with him the exact same message which he had heard from my lips—the gospel. 'I was left feeling that I was wearing dirty dungarees and that I needed a good bath,' he said. My husband and I had a blessed time of fellowship with him and his family over the following year, but towards the close of it he died from a brain tumour. If we only felt more strongly the importance and power of prayer, as well as the wonderful privilege we have in being able to pray for others, we might be found more often on our knees.

## BIG HEART, BIG VISION

God loves to hear His children when they call on Him, and we need to avail ourselves constantly of this means of grace. Intercessory prayer—prayer for other people—is an expression of our concern for others. God is concerned for the people about us; therefore, when we intercede we are, as it were, aligning our concern for them with God's concern. Paul tells us that prayer for all people is good and pleasing to God, whose will it is that all kinds of people will be saved and 'come to a knowledge of the truth' (1 Timothy 2:1–4).

I know a man who, as well as having been a church pastor for a number of years in the UK, became the principal of a theological college and then a professor in another college in the USA. He is very able intellectually; more importantly, he is a spiritually minded man who has a heart for people. He once told the story of how he had been invited to the home of a Muslim because the Muslim wanted to show this pastor 'his box of secrets'. As the evening wore on, the Christian pastor asked the Muslim where the box was. The Muslim touched his chest and said, 'In here.' When the pastor asked why he did not share this with his imam or with a mullah, the man replied, 'Our God has no heart and therefore his servants can have no heart. I cannot share my heart with someone who does not have a heart. But I have discovered that the Christian God has a heart and therefore I think His servants will have a heart too. I can share my heart with a man whose God has a heart.' The question inevitably presses itself upon our consciences: do we have big hearts and big vision, or do we think just of our families, our churches and the vicinities in which we live?

**MANY MOURN**

John Wesley once said that the world was his parish. Few will be called to preach as he did; and fewer still will be called to travel the distances which he covered so that Christ might be made known. But, in another way, the world is *our* parish too, when we pray. 'Your kingdom come, your will be done *on earth*,' is what Jesus taught us to pray. Moreover, the 'world' has come to us with the many migrants who arrive in our land from all over the globe, especially at the present time when there are so many displaced people and refugees. Should they not be high on our prayer list? We have so many encouragements to pray: for all sorts of people in all sorts of conditions. And we are told that we will have that for which we ask when it is in accordance with God's will (Mark 11:24; Luke 11:9; John 14:13–14; 15:7; 1 John 3:22; 5:14–15). We need constantly to plead God's promises. William S. Plumer, the great nineteenth-century Southern States preacher who wrote a huge commentary on the book of Psalms, wrote, 'For more than thirty-five years I have had much intercourse with dying saints and sinners of various ages and conditions. In all that time I have not heard one express regret that he had spent too much time in prayer; I have heard many mourn that they had so seldom visited the throne of grace.'[6]

Better by far to have too much than too little prayer in our lives! Jesus said that we should always pray and not faint. When He was on earth, He was the epitome of what a praying person should be. And He has never stopped praying: even in heaven He intercedes for us continually (Romans 8:34). Prayer is a privilege that God has given to us, and we need to avail ourselves of it. We will miss out on the blessing that God gives us in being co-workers with Christ if we do not intercede for others. God can work without our assistance—He is not restrained or limited in any way by our lack of prayer—but He chooses to allow us to be His co-workers and to use our prayers to accomplish His purposes.

### 'HELL CORNER'

There is a wonderful story of God at work by His Spirit during the 1859 revival in America even when there did not *seem* to be any human channel of intercession. There was a certain group of people in New Hampshire who had

no communication with anybody beyond themselves.
These families are distinguished for their profanity,
wickedness, gambling, and almost every vice. They have
no respect for religious institutions. They are shut out from
all means of grace. They are a reckless, hardened set of
people . . . One of these men was at a neighbour's house,
and while there indulged in the most horrid oaths.[7]

The neighbour said that she was afraid the roof would fall over their heads, so terrible were the profanities which this man uttered. She suggested that it was time they had a 'bit of religion'. This was all done in a 'devil may care' kind of attitude. The man thought it would be a good idea if they had a prayer meeting, and a number agreed.

They got a man to lead the meeting—the only man living in
the neighbourhood who had been a professor of religion. He
was a notorious backslider . . . The time came for the meeting,
and all assembled. The backslider undertook to lead the
meeting, but broke down in his prayer and could not go on.
They undertook to sing, and could not make out anything at
that . . . They sent to a deacon of a church living three miles off,
saying that there was to be a prayer-meeting at Hell Corner—the
common name by which the place was known—on next Sunday

afternoon, and wanted him to come down and conduct it. The deacon thought it was either a hoax or a plan to mob him.[8]

But when he spoke to his neighbour, the neighbour said he would go with him to Hell Corner. So the next Sunday they went and found everyone assembled.

'I had not been there but a few minutes,' said the deacon, 'before I felt that the Spirit was there.' Four or five of these hardened, wretched men were struck under conviction at this first meeting. Another meeting was held, and more were converted . . . The work is going on with amazing power. At the last meeting . . . more than one hundred were present. Here was a case where God's Spirit went before the desires of the people in the region that was blessed. God heard the prayers of His children in other places, or it pleased Him in His sovereign mercy to pour out His Holy Spirit upon this wicked community, and turn sinners from the error of their ways to Himself.'[9]

IT IS GOD'S MEMORIAL THAT IN EVERY GENERATION HE HEARETH PRAYER.[10]

God sometimes demonstrates His power in this way. He can work amongst those who appear to be forgotten, the marginalized of the earth. God would indeed have us pray without ceasing, but at times He wants to remind us that He is sovereign, and He alone saves.

## Food for thought

1. *Have you ever known what it is to be in* an agony of soul *over someone who is unsaved?*
2. *Has God saved others through your witness? If so, how does this encourage you?*
3. *Do you covenant to pray for specific people? Have you*

**HIS TREASURED POSSESSION**

*considered meeting with a prayer partner to encourage
you in this endeavour?*

4. *Do you pray for the many international, and often
displaced, people in our country?*

**Notes**

1 *The Evangelical Magazine of Wales* 18, no. 4 (Aug–Sept. 1979).

2 Ibid.

3 Spurgeon, *Early Years*, 155. Some of Spurgeon's prayers were written down
(no doubt in shorthand!) by hearers and have been published in C. H.
Spurgeon, *The Pastor in Prayer* (Edinburgh: Banner of Truth Trust, 2004
[1893]).

4 Introduction to John Flavel, *The Mystery of Providence* (Edinburgh: Banner of
Truth Trust, 1963 [1678]), p. 11. The account is also given by Robert Murray
M'Cheyne, who tells us that Short was still working on his farm at the age of
100! Although he had lived in spiritual carelessness and sin, he went on to
live to 116 and gave every evidence of having been born again: Robert
Murray M'Cheyne, *The Works of the Late Robert Murray M'Cheyne*, Vol. 2
(New York: Robert Carter, 1847), pp. 221–222.

5 As a one-time Presbyterian minister, Flavel would have followed *The
Westminster Directory for the Public Worship of God*. This directory gives
detailed instruction for prayer to be offered for God's blessing of His truth to
the people gathered.

6 Quoted in Prime, *Power of Prayer*, p. 244.

7 Ibid., p. 76.

8 Ibid., p. 77.

9 Ibid., pp. 77–78.

10 Ibid., p. 260.

# Part 4. Value for the present and for the life to come

# 22 A countless number: value for the present life

*But when the kindness and love of God our Saviour appeared, he saved us, not because of righteous things we had done, but because of his mercy. He saved us through the washing of rebirth and renewal by the Holy Spirit, whom he poured out on us generously through Jesus Christ our Saviour, so that, having been justified by his grace, we might become heirs having the hope of eternal life. (Titus 3:4–7)*

*Blessed assurance, Jesus is mine!*
*O what a foretaste of glory divine!*
*Heir of salvation, purchase of God,*
*Born of His Spirit, washed in His blood. (Fanny Crosby)*

How easy it is for us only to value things once they have been taken from us! And it is frequently the things we may not value highly which prove to be the very things that help us keep to our course. People who have suffered hardship and difficulties through persecution because they have lived for Christ have often testified to the fact that, time and again, such providences have made Christ all the more real to them. God, by His Spirit, reminds them that they are not alone in their suffering (1 Peter 5:9).

One of the biggest blights on Christian living in the West today is individualism. We are surrounded by those who believe that they can be saved from their sins and then live with little or minimal reference to the body of Christ, the church. This may well be part of the 'carry over' or 'baggage' brought from the pre-Christian life into the new life. Since society in the West has, generally speaking, become individualistic, it is hardly surprising that the church experiences the impact of this when people are newly converted. God does not intend that His children should survive alone in a hostile world—not when they can be safe within Christ's sheepfold. We are His body, and He must be saddened to see His people wandering from the secure boundaries of His care and protection. The Lord never intended us to 'go it alone'. His intention was always to build His church, 'living stone' by 'living stone', every believer adding to the lustre of the whole. Our mandate is to advance like an army, with the Captain of our salvation leading the way, not to be like deserters wishing to leave the battlefield.

O Church, arise, and put your armour on;
Hear the call of Christ our Captain.
For now the weak can say that they are strong
In the strength that God has given.
With shield of faith and belt of truth,
We'll stand against the devil's lies;
An army bold, whose battle-cry is Love,
Reaching out to those in darkness.[1]

We are meant to die for one another! 'My command is this: love each other as I have loved you. Greater love has no one than this: to lay down one's life for one's friends' (John 15:12–13).

**OUR TURN**
The privilege and blessings of being saved are immense, and

the delight at being part of the universal church of Christ should flood us with unspeakably great joy and be a great source of pleasure to us. We are not on our own: we are part of a countless number of those who have lived through the centuries and borne a faithful testimony to Jesus Christ. Now we in our turn need to follow faithfully every dictate and command of our Saviour. We are to love our brothers and sisters in the church, living in harmony with them despite our many foibles. 'Just as a body, though one, has many parts, but all its many parts form one body, so it is with Christ. For we . . . form one body' (1 Corinthians 12:12–13a).

We are to be His representatives on earth, living in unity with one another, and in so doing proclaim by our actions to those who are impervious to the claims of Christ that we support and love each other. Of course, it is far easier, in one sense, not to have any accountability to someone else. But this was never the Lord's intention for His people. If we are not settled locally in a church, how can we know the privilege of correction (see Matthew 18:15–17)? We can become like loose cannons and laws to ourselves.

### WIFI

When Saul was persecuting the church and Christ met with Him, He did not say to Saul, 'Why are you persecuting those who believe in Me?' but 'Why do you persecute Me?' (see Acts 9:4). We, the church, are His body on earth, but we cannot be identified as such if we never meet with His people. We need to be not only in the church and of it, but asking ourselves where we fit into the whole. I remember a pastor once employing the acronym WIFI ('Where I Fit In') to challenge us to determine for ourselves what our role in the church was to be! What does God want us to do? What are our marching orders? We are to proclaim Christ: the merits of His life, the glory of His death and resurrection, and the assertion of His marvellous ascension; to tell out the great wonders of our Saviour, who makes shattered lives new and whole. We are to compel people to come in and to know this life-changing experience. The compulsion we use is not, of course, the brute force which, sadly, has sometimes been employed by well-meaning (and not-so-well-meaning) folk and which characterizes certain sub-Christian sects and other religious groups; rather, it is to be the compulsion of love and a holy example.

## SERIOUS INVOLVEMENT

I doubt if anyone would believe us if we said we were faithful members of a particular society yet, after paying our subscription, we hardly attended a meeting. If there is no serious involvement, there is no serious interest. Only one conclusion can be drawn: there is no heart or conviction attached to our membership. And this is exactly the inference that will be drawn concerning our profession about following Christ if we are not involved with His church: one could only conclude that the Jesus we are following in such a half-hearted and uncommitted way is not the Jesus of the Bible, the Jesus who has brought us out of darkness and into His wonderful light.

In one of our house moves I was overwhelmed by the kindness of many people, but I distinctly remember two particular individuals. One, a member of the church, brought us a lovely plant and meal, but during the weeks that followed I looked in vain for her in church. The other exceedingly helpful person was a man who assembled and screwed into place all my curtain poles and did the hundred-and-one other practical jobs which attend a move and which would have taken my husband double the time this dear brother needed to complete the tasks. In conversation with him I asked him about his wife and discovered that she was unconverted. Again, over the coming weeks I felt saddened by his absence from church. When he finally reappeared at church after about six weeks, there seemed to be no mitigating circumstances to justify his long absence, nor did he offer any explanation for this.

In the case of the woman, her attendance at church proved almost non-existent; in the case of the man, my husband waited for the right moment and spoke to him about the fact that his lack of passion to be with his church family was bound to have an impact upon his unconverted wife. Why should she take seriously the claims of Christ when her husband appeared to have such little commitment to God's people as a whole in their gatherings? I once heard a pastor say that the church resembles a football match: one set of people in desperate need of rest, watched by twenty thousand people in desperate need of exercise! Similarly, the lack of commitment on the part of this man who was absent for six weeks probably spoke volumes (negatively) to his wife! (In the goodness and mercy of God, things changed dramatically after my husband challenged him.)

Is this true of us? Do we give people reason to think that there is little, if any, worth or benefit in meeting with brothers and sisters, much less being committed to them? We can be sure of one thing: if our meeting with God's people becomes intermittent, and if when we do meet with them we head for the door as soon as the final 'Amen' is said, not only will we be missing out, but also we will be a definite 'turn-off' with respect to the gospel for anyone who has become interested enough in gospel matters to meet with us. The late Douglas MacMillan—one-time shepherd of four-legged sheep and then for many years a greatly beloved shepherd of the two-legged variety of 'sheep' in his home country of Scotland—said that just after he was converted he learned a very important lesson from his father concerning Christian fellowship being a means of grace to the believer:

We were doing something in the smithy on the farm, and the fire on the blacksmith's hearth was alight with little lumps of coal. I was turning the handle, blowing the bellows, doing the hard graft, and he said, 'Douglas, I want you to look at something.' With a pair of tongs he took just one coal off the fire, put it on the anvil and said, 'Watch that!' It came out glowing red, almost white, and we stood and watched it . . . It began to turn blue, greeny-blue, and then black. He said, 'If we leave it long enough, it will be cold. Always seek Christian fellowship.'[2]

We need one another in order to stay red-hot and fervent in our joy and service of Christ and in our service of one another. We can easily become distracted: dallying with the world, we may end up making all sorts of compromises. We need one another in order to stay the course and remain true. And it is vital for us to learn from the Word of God *in fellowship with each other*, as well as on our own.

## A HEALTHY SPIRITUAL LIFE

What are the benefits we enjoy by being part of the living, vibrant body of Christ? God has given us the means by which divine grace is imparted to our souls and by which our growth in grace is promoted. And this is how grace can be appropriated: by hearing the Word of God (among His people!) both preached and sung (as well as reading it in private); by prayer, whether private or public; and by the sacraments—the Lord's Supper and baptism. God's grace is known and experienced through these 'exercises'. These means are laid down in Scripture as marks of a healthy spiritual life: 'They devoted themselves to the apostles' teaching and to fellowship, to the breaking of bread and to prayer' (Acts 2:42).

We cannot hope to grow as Christians if we are not using those means which God has appointed to enable us to grow. That is why, if we are really serious about our development and maturity as children of God, we cannot be half-hearted about hearing God's Word preached or being present at the Lord's Supper. Neither can we just be present for the preaching, as some are in the habit of doing. If the Word of God is being sung in the form of hymns and psalms, we are failing to receive the grace God imparts through such means if we slip into a meeting just to hear the preacher.

If we have the liberty to meet with one another, we are a privileged people. How we should take every opportunity to meet together in order to strengthen one another's hands!

And let us consider how we may spur one another on towards love and good deeds, not giving up meeting together, as some are in the habit of doing, but encouraging one another—and all the more as you see the Day approaching. (Hebrews 10:24–25)

## Food for thought

1. *How important is it for professing Christians to be part of the visible church?*
2. *What effect does our lack of church attendance have on:*
   - *Our families?*
   - *Non-Christians—if they know we are professing Christians?*
3. *Why do we need one another in a church?*
4. *What are the benefits and privileges of being part of a church?*

### Notes

1 Stuart Townend and Keith Getty, 'O Church, Arise'.

2 MacMillan, *Lord Our Shepherd*, pp. 49–50.

# 23 Our ultimate goal: value for the life to come

*Then I saw 'a new heaven and a new earth', for the first heaven and the first earth had passed away, and there was no longer any sea. I saw the Holy City, the new Jerusalem, coming down out of heaven from God, prepared as a bride beautifully dressed for her husband. (Revelation 21:1–2)*

*One drop of the sweetness of heaven is enough to take away all the sourness and bitterness of all the afflictions in the world. (Jeremiah Burroughs)*

Many Christians believe that when we die we will reach our *ultimate goal*: heaven! But Christ did not save us just for *heaven*; He saved us primarily for Himself. 'Our Saviour is not content that we should merely have heaven or love or glory. He wills that we should have Him. For to a believer Christ is more than heaven and His presence better than crowns, thrones or diadems of splendour.'[1]

And Christ, the Bridegroom, will one day be returning to claim His Bride. I have attended quite a number of weddings, but not once have I seen the bride preoccupied with the venue! Her eye is firmly fixed on her beloved. Likewise for us, it will not be heaven with which we will be enraptured when we reach it, but looking on our 'dear Bridegroom's face'.[2] Indeed, care is needed here. Death is the gateway to an 'intermediate state'. The final goal, the 'endgame', will be when our bodies are resurrected and, together with the heavenly Bridegroom, we come with Him to a renewed earth: heaven and earth will have been joined.

## GUNPOWDER RATHER THAN GOD

We have seen in the previous chapters that our fight is against our fleshly sin, the world and the devil: but in this new heaven and new earth sin will be no more and will not cloud our vision or actions. There we will be occupied with all that God has in store for us, but it will not distract us from Him in all His glory: our eyes will be ever upon our God; He will be the light by which we walk (Revelation 21:23). We must thank God for freeing us from a life that was destroying us; we were enslaved by sin and the devil, but now we have been set free and have set our sails for heaven. But here on earth, our fight is not yet at an end. We are so often engrossed in the battle, and can become so weary of the war, that we are sometimes more conscious of the 'gunpowder' than of God; we can be so absorbed in the world that the frothiness of life hides His face from view. In whatever position we find ourselves, we need to *keep looking up!* Our prayers and our lives should be shaped in the light of an eternal perspective. Am I living in anticipation of that great day?

## JOSTLING FOR OUR ATTENTION

As we have seen, we should seek to be the best we can be in whatever roles we occupy, and this will, of course, mean that we should be conscientious in our work and in the care of our families, as well as in being responsible citizens in the communities in which we live. In addition to these areas of life, there are a multitude of legitimate 'extras' that can jostle for our time and attention. These can all be good things, but we need considerable organizational skills to fit all of them into our busy lives. God has given us a wonderful world: all around us is a vast array of delights He has given us in nature, art, literature, and many other areas. With such a range of occupations, duties and interests, we need to be ultra-organized if we are to put each in its right place and keep each in proportion, and not fritter our time away on non-essentials.

Our technological age is a tremendous boon to us. It has helped in many ways. Women no longer have to spend whole days washing clothes, scrubbing floors and carrying out back-breaking tasks in the home. But we may find that the time that has been saved is being drained away in hours spent on the Internet, Instagram, Facebook or even games on our phones: so many distractions that we really have no time at all to 'look up'! The devil does not mind us turning up at church once a week or once a month; that single appearance (with no attendance at times when God's people meet for prayer, whether in a homegroup or as the whole church) is not going to dent his kingdom in the least. As long as he can keep our eyes firmly fixed on earth and captivated by it, with minimal reference to God, his strategy has succeeded.

### 'PRACTISE SELF-INDULGENCE'

One of the devil's greatest tactics is to enfeeble Christians, especially those of us who are 'retired' (and many in that category today are younger than sixty-five!), by encouraging us to be so preoccupied with planning holidays that we cannot find time to think of much else! I heard of one Christian woman who, on her return from a holiday, was already discussing where she would spend her next break! Packer expresses the need to assess where we are and to evaluate our usefulness. With regard to retired folk, he sums up the world's attitude towards their newly acquired lifestyle:

Relax. Slow down. Take it easy. Amuse yourself. Do only what you enjoy. You are not required to run things anymore, or to exercise any form of creativity, or to take responsibility for guiding and sustaining goal-oriented enterprises. You are off the treadmill and out of the rat race. Now at last, you are your own man (or woman) and can concentrate on having fun. You have your pension; health services are there to look after your body; and club, trips, outings, tours, competitions, games, parties and entertainments are provided in abundance to help you pass the time. So go ahead and practise self-indulgence up to the limit. Fill your life with novelties and hobbies, anything and everything that will hold your interest.[3]

God certainly wants us to enjoy the wonderful world He has made, and He is definitely not a killjoy—He 'richly provides us with everything for our enjoyment' (1 Timothy 6:17b)—but He never intended our pleasure and satisfaction in life to anchor us so forcibly to this earth and to be found only in things. God wants us to *keep looking up*. We are to remind ourselves constantly that our goal and destination lie with our King in heaven! Are we expending as much energy in our preparation for that great trip as we do in our travel arrangements in this world? There is a great amount of hype over getting ready for holidays: things that we need to take with us; injections we need to have if we are going to far-flung places; appropriate clothing; buckets and spades for the children if we are going on beach holidays; sun and mosquito protection; good walking shoes for mountaineers—on and on the list goes, until we hit exhaustion point with all our preparations.

## A BIT MORE 'FROSTING'

A court jester was once asked by a king if he could try on his hat. 'Oh no, your Majesty,' he replied, 'you can only try this on when you prove to be as big a fool as I am.' Sometime later, the king became very ill and was on his deathbed. He called for his jester, who asked the king if he was 'prepared' for *this* journey. 'No,' came the king's sad reply. 'Well, you had better take my hat,' said the jester, 'because you have proved to be a bigger fool than I am.' Are we as foolish? Do we think that being a Christian is just about believing certain things, dropping into church when the fancy takes us and living a 'good' life? We may have a bit more 'frosting' on top of those basics, but the flaw in our beliefs may perhaps only come home to us when it is too late. It is not enough to say we believe, and to go through the motions of a Christian life; we must live authentic, Christlike, Spirit-filled lives, changed on the inside as well as on the outside.

## 'TRUMP OF THE ANGEL'

We are told in Scripture that if we profess to be Christians, certain things follow as surely as day follows night. The first Epistle of John is very instructive with regard to these essential hallmarks in our lives.[4] We may not always be able to see them as clearly ourselves, but we should be able to recognize them in each other. One of these hallmarks is our delight in contemplating the Lord's return:

But, Lord, 'tis for Thee, for Thy coming we wait,
The sky, not the grave, is our goal;
Oh, trump of the angel! Oh, voice of the Lord!
Blessed hope, blessed rest of my soul![5]

It is for Christ's Second Coming we watch and wait—and for which we long: to see Him not as He was when on earth, derided by all but His own, but as the Glorious King. Every eye will see Him; and none will scorn Him then.

For the Lord himself will come down from heaven, with a loud command, with the voice of the archangel and with the trumpet call of God, and the dead in Christ will rise first. After that, we who are still alive and are left will be caught up together with them in the clouds to meet the Lord in the air. And so we will be with the Lord for ever. (1 Thessalonians 4:16–17)

We are to encourage each other with these words. *This is our ultimate goal*: to see the Lord Jesus Christ and to live with Him for ever in that new heaven and new earth which has been prepared for us. How often do we think of the Lord's return? We constantly need to remind ourselves that we are just lodging here, because 'our citizenship is in heaven' (Philippians 3:20).[6] Philippians 3:20–21 continues, 'And we eagerly await a Saviour from there, the Lord Jesus Christ, who, by the power that enables him to bring everything under his control, will transform our lowly bodies so that they will be like his glorious body.' Do we eagerly await Him? 'He will appear a second time, not to bear sin, but to bring salvation to those who are *waiting* for him' (Hebrews 9:28b).

## EYES FIXED ON HOME

Once, on our return journey from visiting a missionary family in Sicily, we had a very long train ride and then had to find somewhere to stay overnight at Catania in Sicily. We had no idea where to lodge, so enquired at the Tourist Information Centre. We were directed to a small hotel, and to this day we are not quite sure what sort of establishment it was: our passports were taken, and we began to wonder if we would ever get them back. (We were, after all, in the home base of the mafia!) In the corridor there were a number of scantily dressed women leaning against walls and doorways, and when we found our room we were horrified to discover bugs in the bed and a general shabbiness. As we had but a few hours before we had to leave again, we decided to sleep in the armchairs. Due to the constant clamour around us, we were only able to doze on and off. We were very relieved when we were finally on our way to the airport! How thankful we were that we had no reason to prolong our stay there! Our eyes and expectations were firmly fixed on home.

## ONLY TEMPORARY

On another occasion, when my husband and I were visiting friends in Germany, we had an overnight stop in London before catching our flight early the next day. My husband had been in London with work the month before and, thanks to a good deal he found on the Internet, had stayed very cheaply in quite an exclusive hotel at Canary Wharf. So this time he mentioned to the receptionist that he had had a delightful room during his previous stay, and 'would she be able to match it?' To our great delight, we were given quite an exceptional room. We had not only a king-size bed, but our very own lounge that overlooked the river! Wonderful! However, we did not attempt to settle down as we were only staying a short time; we certainly had no time to unpack our cases. However attractive, that hotel room was not our goal. Our aim was Germany and being reunited with our friends.

With respect to our stay in Catania, we certainly did not fall in love with the hotel or cry when we had to leave! And, although the hotel at Canary Wharf was lavish, I am sure my husband would have been quite rightly concerned if the next morning I had refused to leave, wanting to spend my holiday in the confines of those four walls! However attractive the surroundings were, our stay was only temporary. So whether our circumstances are unattractive and disagreeable or impressive and cosy, we need to remind ourselves that life is fleeting, and we are here only for a very short time.

The world is a great inn; we are guests in this inn. Travellers, when they are met in their inn, do not spend all their time in speaking about the inn; they are to lodge there but a few hours and are gone. They speak about their home and the country to which they are travelling. So when we meet together, we should not be talking only about the world; we are to leave this presently. We should talk about our heavenly country.[7]

This world in its present form is not our home, and so we are never to set down roots and live as though we were staying here for ever. That way of thinking characterizes the world, not those who are pilgrims journeying to 'a better country' (Hebrews 11:16). This place is just a stopover until we reach our permanent home. There may be many trials and hardships on the way, even times when we feel we can hardly go on; but when we reach those shores, all will be forgotten in the glory that awaits us.

When ye are come to the other side of the water, and have set down your foot on the shore of glorious eternity, and look back again to the waters and to your wearisome journey, and shall see in that clear glass of endless glory, nearer to the bottom of God's wisdom, ye shall then be forced to say, 'If God had done otherwise with me than He hath done, I had never come to the enjoyment of this crown of glory.'[8]

## ETERNITY IS WAITING

Yet our danger is that we cannot see past our circumstances, and we can fail to see God's good hand in them all, weaning us from this world. It has been said that it took just one night for the Israelites to get out of Egypt, but it took forty years or more to get Egypt out of the Israelites! We can be so taken up with the 'now' that we cannot see beyond our present situation. We need to remind ourselves that this is not our all: eternity is waiting. 'If you should see a man shut up in a closed room, idolizing a set of lamps and rejoicing in their light, and you wished to make him truly happy, you would begin by blowing out all his lamps; and then throw open the shutters to let in the light of heaven.'[9]

The Lord has given us great encouragements to help us focus our gaze upon the new heaven and the new earth and His glorious coming. But we will only look with delight and wait for the day of His return if we are not simply *looking* but also *living* for Christ. 'When Christ, *who is your life*, appears, then you also will appear with him in glory' (Colossians 3:4). One of the greatest consolations of that day will be that our sin will trouble us no more, for '*we shall be like him*, for we shall see him as he is' (1 John 3:2b). No more sin, sorrow or sloth! Packer, writing on 2 Corinthians 5, has a very sobering word to say about our life with Christ in eternity:

The quality of our unending enjoyment of Christ's love and goodness will in some way correspond to the quality of love and devotion to Him that marks our lives now (5:10). [Paul's] reference to knowing 'the fear of the Lord' (5:11) then hints at the sad possibility that slackness and irresponsibility in Christ's service now might unfit one for the fullest fullness of heaven's joy.[10]

### BETTER AND LASTING POSSESSIONS

God has given us abundant incentives in His Word: we not only possess Christ, but we have an *inheritance* awaiting us that will never be taken away. 'What kind of people ought [we] to be? [We] ought to live holy and godly lives' (2 Peter 3:11b) when we think of all that we have in Christ. Peter also tells us of that which, on the basis of what is now ours, *will* be our possession:

In [God's] great mercy he has given us new birth into a living hope through the resurrection of Jesus Christ from the dead, and into an *inheritance that can never perish, spoil or fade*. This inheritance is kept in heaven for you, who through faith are shielded by God's power until the coming of the salvation that is ready to be revealed in the last time. (1 Peter 1:3–5)

What a prospect we have as believers, and what riches we have in our Lord Jesus! Hebrews 10:34b tells us that we have 'better and lasting possessions'. If God is *our treasured possession*, we have treasure indeed! When we are absorbed and preoccupied with this world to the exclusion of Christ, we are like the babies and toddlers we sometimes see at Christmas time who are taken up with the wrapping paper enclosing their presents rather than with the presents themselves. God has given us so many blessings on this earth which He wants us to enjoy, but He does not want us to be so absorbed in them that we lose sight of the great treasure trove that is ours in Him. 'I have treasured the words of his mouth more than my daily bread' (Job 23:12b).

## NOT MEDIOCRE

Our problem is that we can be so taken up with the immediate, and the treasure we are storing up for ourselves on earth, that we lose sight of our spiritual treasure. We can become so accustomed to the trinkets we find around us that true Christian gems gradually lose their attraction. Treasure of *real* worth begins to be devalued. We are satisfied with costume jewellery instead of the genuine article. God has told us He will give us 'hidden treasures, riches stored in secret places, so that you may know that I am the LORD . . . who summons you by name' (Isaiah 45:3). We need to start looking for this 'hidden treasure'. God wants to give us the best in life, not that which is mediocre or counterfeit.

The 'dairyman's daughter' knew all about this 'best in life'. She was a young woman in the late eighteenth to early nineteenth century who had much to teach those around her, lessons we need to take to heart today. She had found that 'hidden treasure':

If we could but fix our eyes always on that crown of glory that waits us in the skies, we should never grow weary in well-doing; but should run with patience and delight in the work and ways of God, where He appoints us. We should not then, as we frequently do, suffer these trifling objects here on earth to draw away our minds from God, to rob Him of His glory, and our souls of that happiness and comfort which the believer may enjoy amidst outward afflictions . . . If I am not deceived, I wish myself to enjoy His gracious favour, more than all the treasures which earth can afford . . . that they may not have power on my heart to draw or attract it from God, who is worthy of my highest esteem, and of all my affections.[11]

## SENT ON AHEAD

Our hearts can be so bound up with things that they can take us away from God and all He has to give us of Himself. If we can but see past the here and now, we will be able to embrace true riches, glorious treasure. The following challenging excerpt comes from the chapter 'Eyes on Eternity' in Randy Alcorn's book *The Treasure Principle*:

The streets of Cairo were hot and dusty. Pat and Rakel Thurman took us down an alley. We drove past Arabic signs to a gate that opened to a plot of overgrown grass. It was a graveyard for American missionaries. As my family and I followed, Pat pointed to a sun-scorched tombstone that read: 'William Borden, 1887–1913.' Borden, a Yale graduate and heir to a great wealth, rejected a life of ease in order to bring the gospel to Muslims. Refusing even to buy himself a car, Borden gave away hundreds of thousands of dollars to missions. After only four months of zealous ministry in Egypt, he contracted spinal meningitis and died at the age of twenty-five. I dusted off the epitaph on Borden's grave. After describing his love and sacrifices for the kingdom of God and for Muslim people, the inscription ended with a phrase I've never forgotten: 'Apart from faith in Christ, there is no explanation for such a life.' The Thurmans took us straight from Borden's grave to the Egyptian National Museum. The King Tut exhibit was mind-boggling. Tutankhamun, the boy king, was only seventeen when he died. He was buried with solid gold chariots and thousands of golden artefacts. His gold coffin was found with gold tombs within gold tombs within gold tombs. The burial site was filled with tons of gold. The Egyptians believed in an afterlife—one where they could take earthly treasures. But all the treasures intended for King Tut's eternal enjoyment stayed right where they were until Howard Carter discovered the burial chamber in 1922. They hadn't been touched for more than three thousand years. I was struck by the contrast between these two graves. Borden's was obscure, dusty, and hidden off the back alley of a street littered with garbage. Tutankhamun's tomb glittered with unimaginable wealth. Yet where are these two young men now? One, who lived in opulence and called himself king, is in the misery of a Christless eternity. The other, who lived a modest life on earth in service of the one true King, is enjoying his everlasting reward in the presence of his Lord. Tut's life was tragic because of an awful truth discovered too late—he couldn't take his treasures with him. William Borden's life was triumphant. Why? Because, instead of leaving his treasures, he sent them on ahead.[12]

**A WOODEN HUT**

What sort of treasure are we living for, and how much are we sending on ahead? The story is told of a man who died and arrived at the gates of heaven. As he was ushered in he was overcome by the incomparable quality of the mansions all around him: they were magnificent! As he was guided through the streets by an angel, he found himself amongst dwellings which were not quite as splendid as the ones they had just left behind, but were still exceedingly impressive.

Another street brought them to smaller dwellings, but still quite grand. Soon, after travelling along a few more streets, they came to a patch of ground upon which was a wooden hut. The man was perplexed and looked to the angel for an explanation. The angel said, 'I'm afraid this is all we could manage in relation to what you sent on ahead!'

We are categorically told not to store up treasure on earth (although in Christ 'there dwells a treasure all divine, and matchless grace has made that treasure mine');[13] in contrast, we are told emphatically to store up treasure for ourselves in heaven. God knows our hearts; He knows if we are wedded to this world. The Bible warns us that 'what people value highly is detestable in God's sight' (Luke 16:15). Our real treasure should be inward and eternal, not bound up in what is temporal and will soon pass away.

Worldliness is one of the greatest dangers that beset man's soul . . . they 'lay up treasure on earth', and forget to 'lay up treasure in heaven'. May we all remember this! Where are our hearts? What do we love best? Are our chiefest affections on things in earth, or things in heaven? Life or death depends on the answer we can give to these questions. If our treasure is earthly, our hearts will be earthly also. 'Where your treasure is, there will your heart be.'[14]

### THE SHEER JOY OF PERFORMING

Jesus takes note of every kind act we perform, even the seemingly most insignificant (Matthew 10:42). God is keeping a record of all these deeds: how we treat, help, encourage and support others—with our time, talents and possessions (including money). Malachi 3:16 describes how 'a scroll of remembrance was written in [God's] presence concerning those who feared the LORD and honoured his name'. God gives us further motivation to lay up our treasures for eternity. Both Timothy (2 Timothy 4:8) and Peter tell us of the 'crown' we will be given: 'And when the Chief Shepherd appears, you will receive the *crown of glory* that will never fade away' (1 Peter 5:4). And when Christ comes He will bring with Him His rewards, which He will present to His loved ones: 'Look, I am coming soon! My *reward* is with me, and I will give to each person according to what they have done' (Revelation 22:12).

We sometimes shy away from the subject of rewards. We may feel totally unworthy, and we may rightly regard that having Christ and all that is ours in Him is more than enough to motivate us to labour for His glory. But the fact is that it is Jesus who has told us of rewards; therefore, we need to take heed to what He has said. Colossians 3:24 reminds us, 'you know that you will receive an inheritance from the Lord as a reward. It is the Lord Christ you are serving.' Our problem may lie in the fact that we are viewing these 'rewards' in somewhat of a worldly way. When little children tidy their rooms, because they have been good and obedient, they may get some pocket money: their reward is an incentive for them to do what they should do. We should rather view our heavenly reward like the reward of the child who is told to practise the piano, and after years and years of expended energy becomes the pianist *par excellence*. That child's reward is the sheer joy of performing, the result of determined and rigorous application. We are told in Matthew 16:27, 'the Son of Man is going to come in his Father's glory with

**HIS TREASURED POSSESSION**

his angels, and then he will reward each person according to what they have done'—saint and sinner (Romans 2:5–6) alike. Are there degrees of reward in heaven? We have not the space to discuss that here; rather, what we need to remember is 'Whatever you do, work at it with all your heart, as working for the Lord' (Colossians 3:23–24). We are to be faithful in our service for our King, and leave all remuneration to Him.

## THE GREAT FINALE

As we employ our time on earth in obedience to our Master, seeking to be more and more like Him, we live in readiness, watching and waiting for that great finale in heaven. And until that glorious day, we practise on, and on, and on. We show we are part of this heavenly gathering by loving and by living out our part in this earthly gathering; we live just where we are, doing what God has called us to do, loving our own and all those He has placed in our little worlds; being faithful to Him, enjoying the world He has given us, but at the same time keeping our eyes on eternity, continually looking up. There we 'will sparkle in his land like jewels in a crown. How attractive and beautiful [we] will be!' (Zechariah 9:16b–17a). As we approach that finishing line, we will need to remind ourselves that our exertions have not been for an earthly prize, but for an incorruptible crown: *Christ, our treasured possession*, will be ours for all eternity!

On Christ and what he has done, my soul hangs for time and eternity! And if your soul also hangs there, it will be saved as surely as mine shall be! And if you are lost trusting in Christ . . . I will be lost with you—and I will go to Hell with you! I must do so, for I have nothing else to rely upon

**HIS TREASURED POSSESSION**

but the fact that Jesus Christ, the Son of God, lived, died, was buried, rose again and went up to Heaven—and still lives and pleads for sinners at the right hand of God![15]

## Food for thought

1. *What is your ultimate goal?*

2. *Why is God's face sometimes hidden from view?*

3. *What do you need to cultivate to help you amidst all the things that jostle for your time? Do you sometimes dissipate your time?*

4. *What is one of the greatest strategies of the devil to enfeeble us, especially retired Christians?*

5. *What are the hallmarks of the life of the Christian?*

6. *Do you live as though you are merely lodging here, or are you too earthbound?*

7. *Do you contemplate the Lord's return, and do you live in the light of His return?*

8. *What is the treasure for which you are living? Are you sending your treasure on ahead of you to heaven? Is your treasure being stored up in heaven or on earth?*

9. *Are you looking forward to heaven, and are you prepared to die?*

### Notes

1   Roberts, *Thought of God*, p. 82.

2   From Anne Ross Cousin's hymn 'The Sands of Time Are Sinking'.

3   Packer, *Finishing Our Course with Joy*, p. 27.

4   See Appendix 13, 'Hallmarks of the Christian'.

**5**   Horatio G. Spafford, 'When Peace Like. River'.

**6**   The following article takes up this theme: Andrew Davies, 'Time and Eternity: The Puritan Outlook', in *Westminster Conference 1999: God Is Faithful*, Puritan Papers (Stoke-on-Trent: Westminster Conference, 2000), p 49.

**7**   Watson, *Christian Soldier*, p. 69.

**8**   Samuel Rutherford, quoted in Gilbert, *Dictionary*, p. 265.

**9**   Eareckson Tada, *Heaven*, p. 259.

**10**   Packer, *Finishing Our Course with Joy*, p. 90.

**11**   Richmond, *Dairyman's Daughter*, pp. 26, 36.

**12**   Alcorn, *Treasure Principle*, pp. 36–40.

**13**   From William Gadsby's hymn 'Immortal Honours Rest on Jesus' Head'.

**14**   Ryle, *Expository Thoughts on St Matthew*, p. 56.

**15**   C. H. Spurgeon, 'A Bold Challenge Justified', Sermon no. 3067 (delivered 1871), Christian Classics Ethereal Library, http://www.ccel.org/ccel/spurgeon/sermons53.xlvii.html.

# Appendix 1.
# What is godliness?

The following excerpts on godliness are from Thomas Watson, *The Godly Man's Picture*:

Godliness is the sacred impression and workmanship of God in a man, whereby from being carnal he is made spiritual . . .

What a rare thing godliness is! It is not airy and puffed up, but solid, and such as will take up the heart and spirits. Godliness consists in an exact harmony between holy principles and practices . . . So sublime is godliness that it cannot be delineated in its perfect radiance and lustre, though an angel should take the pencil . . . Godliness is a spiritual queen, and whoever marries her is sure of a large dowry with her . . . Godliness puts a man in heaven before his time. Christian, aspire after piety; it is a lawful ambition. Look at the saints' characteristics here and never leave off until you have got them stamped upon your own soul. This is the grand business which should swallow up your time and thoughts.[1]

**Note**

1 Watson, *Godly Man's Picture*, pp. 12, 7–8.

# Appendix 2.
# Thomas Watson and how to live a godly life

### THE MARKS OF GODLINESS

They can be summarized in the following way:

- *One who is growing towards God* in Knowledge, Faith, Love, Character and Worship.
- *One who delights in Christ* not human approval, in passion for Christ's glory, in Christ's Word and in Christ's Spirit.
- *One who is growing in humility* through dependence upon prayer, focus on Heaven, patience, thanksgiving, love for the saints and self-sacrifice.
- *One who is practical in his religion:* good to individuals, a doer of spiritual works, trained in religion, walking with God and striving to be an instrument for making others godly.[1]

### Note

1  Quoted from Jenkins, 'Thomas Watson and How to Live a Godly Life', p 29.

# Appendix 3.
# 'Lean Hard' by
# Octavius Winslow

Child of my love, lean hard,
And let me feel the pressure of your care;
I know your burden, child.
I shaped it;
Poised it in my own hand;
Made no proportion in its weight
To your unaided strength,
For even as I laid it on, I said,
'I shall be near, and while she leans on me,
This burden shall be mine, not hers;
So shall I keep my child
Within the circling arms of my own love.'
Here, lay it down, nor fear
To impose it on a shoulder which upholds
The government of worlds.
Yet closer come; you are not near enough.
I would embrace your care;
So I might feel my child reposing on my breast.
You love me? I knew it. Doubt not then;
But loving me, lean hard.[1]

**Note**

1   Quoted from Cowman, *Streams in the Desert*, p. 267.

# Appendix 4.
# 'One Day' by Mary Butterfield

One day when walking down the street,
On business bent, while thinking hard
About the 'hundred cares' which seemed
Like thunder clouds about to break
In torrents, Self-Pity said to me:
'You poor, poor thing, you have too much
To do. Your life is far too hard.
This heavy load will crush you soon.'
A swift response of sympathy
Welled up within . . .
'Ah, yes, it will break and crush my life;
I cannot bear this constant strain
Of endless, aggravating cares;
They are too great for such as I.'
So thus my heart consoled itself,
'Enjoying misery', when lo!
A 'still small voice' distinctly said,
''Twas sent to lift you—not to crush.'
I saw at once my great mistake.
My place was not beneath the load
But on the top! God meant it not
That I should carry it. He sent
It here to carry me. Full well
He knew my incapacity
Before the plan was made. He saw
A child of His in need of grace
And power to serve; a puny twig
Requiring sun and rain to grow;

An undeveloped chrysalis;
A weak soul lacking faith in God.
He could not help but see all this
And more. And then, with tender thought
He placed it where it had to grow—
Or die. To lie and cringe beneath
One's load means death, but life and power
Await all those who dare to arise above.
Our burdens are our wings; on them
We soar to higher realms of grace;
Without them we must ever roam
On plains of undeveloped faith,
(For faith grows but by exercise
In circumstance impossible).
O paradox of Heaven. The load
We think will crush was sent to lift us
Up to God! Then, soul of mine,
Climb up! For naught can e'er be crushed
Save what is underneath the weight.
How may we climb! By what ascent
Will we crest the critical cares
Of life! Within His word is found
The key which opens His secret stairs;
Alone with Christ, secluded there,
We mount our loads, and rest in Him.[1]

**Note**

1   Taken from *Streams in the Desert: 360 Daily Devotional Readings* by L. B.
Cowman, ed. James Reimann. Copyright 1925, 1953, and 1965 by Cowman
Publications, Inc., and Copyright © 1996 by Zondervan. Used by permission
of Zondervan. www.zondervan.com.

# Appendix 5.
# 'The Refiner' by James M. Grey (1851–1935)

He sat by a fire of seven-fold heat,
As He watched by the precious ore,
And closer He bent with a searching gaze
As He heated it more and more.

He knew He had ore that could stand the test,
And He wanted the finest gold
To mould as a crown for the King to wear,
Set with gems with a price untold.

So He laid our gold in the burning fire,
Tho' we fain would have said Him, 'Nay,'
And He watched the dross that we had not seen,
And it melted and passed away.

And the gold grew brighter and yet more bright,
But our eyes were so dim with tears,
We saw but the fire, not the Master's hand,
And questioned with anxious fears.

Yet our gold shone out with a richer glow,
As it mirrored the Form above,
That bent o'er the fire, tho' unseen by us,
With a look of ineffable love.

Can we think that it pleases His loving heart
To cause us a moment's pain?
Ah, no! but He saw through the present cross
The bliss of eternal gain.

So He waited there with a watchful eye,
With a love that is strong and sure,
And His gold did not suffer a bit more heat,
Than was needed to make it pure.[1]

### Note

1 Quoted from Cowman, *Streams in the Desert*, pp. 313–314.

# Appendix 6.
# Sitting at Jesus' feet

During my husband's sabbatical, Pastor Tim Mattox, of the church Stephen and I were then attending in Paphos, Cyprus, *happened* to be preaching the following message. These are a few of his thoughts I managed to scribble down in the course of his sermon. I trust you will be challenged as I was from this teaching, which tallied with the chapter I had just finished writing (ch. 7: 'No Dirty Tools'). So many of the themes in this book were picked up in this one sermon!

### SERMON ON LUKE 10:38–42

We are called the most connected people in our generation, but we have so little quiet, and only slices of peace and quiet in the times in which we live; we are so disconnected from God. We have no time to sit at Jesus' feet. One thing is needed and necessary: to rediscover the joy of sitting at His feet. The world will barge in upon us every day, the devil will throw every distraction in our way. If a magnate in world finance said he could show us a way to become successful and rich, we would give him all our attention and do whatever he said, sparing no time or energy to accomplish what was suggested. However, when Jesus says, 'Only one thing is needed' (Luke 10:42a), we hardly spare Him the time of day. This is the nuts and bolts of Christianity: we need this fellowship with our Saviour—reading and prayer, sitting at Jesus' feet in disciple mode.

The amount of time we spend in the Word of God is an

indicator of our intimacy with our Lord. The Scriptures are alive, and our spiritual inner man needs daily to be made alive. Do we feel cold and empty? This may be an indicator that we are not feeding on the Word of God. A baby is fed by its mother, but we would think there was something dreadfully wrong if we saw a teenager still taking milk from a baby's bottle! Sitting at Jesus' feet and drinking in His Words should be one of our highest priorities. What percentage of time do we give to social media or the television? Does it tally with the time we spend with God? Do I communicate with my Saviour? We need to discipline our lives. Mary chose to sit at Christ's feet; she made the time to be there when many other demands could have tugged her from that place. In our busy lives, we have lists of things that will never go away; we choose them, and then make excuses through those very things, explaining why we cannot spend time with God. We give reasons such as, 'I'll have more time next week/when I feel better/when my children have left home,' and the list goes on and on. Despite the pressures, Mary chose the right thing; and that thing would never be taken away from her. Although Martha appealed to Jesus (as a disciple she was right to go to Him), He directed her to the better thing: that which her sister had chosen.

So much of our lives amounts to nothing. Much of what we do will not last. The time we spend with Christ will not only count but will be rewarded. Where is our treasure, and where are we investing it? We have time only in this world to invest in the one thing that matters: sitting at Jesus' feet. When we arrive in glory and look into Jesus' eyes, will we see a stranger? We should strive for excellence; seeking to achieve is not wrong, but if I lose God in the process, what good is that? Mary loved her Saviour; she was not remembered for her wealth or beauty, as we may not be remembered for our achievements or any great responsibilities we have borne; but like Mary, may our lives be characterized by and remembered for our being those who sat at Jesus' feet. We all have choices to make in life; may we make the right ones. May God be our priority.

# Appendix 7.
# My giving covenant

This covenant comes from Randy Alcon, *The Treasure Principle*.

1. I affirm God's full ownership of me . . . and everything entrusted to me . . .

2. I will set aside the firstfruits—starting with at least 10 percent—of all I receive, treating it as holy and belonging exclusively to the Lord . . .

3. Out of the remaining treasures God entrusts to me, I will seek to make generous freewill gifts . . .

4. I ask God to teach me to give sacrificially to His purposes, including helping the poor and reaching the lost . . .

5. Recognizing that I cannot take earthly treasures from this world, I determine to lay them up as heavenly treasures—for Christ's glory and the eternal good of others and myself . . .[1]

**Note**

1 Alcorn, *Treasure Principle*, p. 96.

# Appendix 8. Treasure principle keys

Giving is a grace just like all the other graces that should characterize our lives as followers of the Lord Jesus Christ. The following extract from Randy Alcorn's book *The Treasure Principle* sets out helpful principles on giving.

Treasure Principle: You can't take it with you—but you can send it on ahead.

### TREASURE PRINCIPLE KEYS

1. *God owns everything. I'm his money manager.* We are the managers of the assets God has entrusted—not given—to us.

2. *My heart always goes where I put God's money.* Watch what happens when you reallocate your money from temporal things to eternal things.

3. *Heaven, not earth, is my home.* We are citizens of a 'better country—a heavenly one' (Hebrews 11:16) . . .

5. *Giving is the only antidote to materialism.* Giving is a joyful surrender to a greater person and a greater agenda. It dethrones me and exalts Him.

6. *God prospers me not to raise my standard of living, but to raise my standard of giving.* God gives us more money than we need so we can give generously.[1]

### Note

1 Alcorn, *Treasure Principle*, p. 95.

**HIS TREASURED POSSESSION**

# Appendix 9.
# 'The Room' by
# Joshua Harris

In that place between wakefulness and dreams, I found myself in the room. There were no distinguishing features save for the mysterious array of black filing cabinets. They were like the ones in libraries that list titles by author or subject in alphabetical order. But these files, which stretched from floor to ceiling and seemingly endlessly in either direction, had very different headings. As I drew near the wall of files, the first to catch my attention was one that read 'Girls I Have Liked'. I opened it and began flipping through the cards. I quickly shut it, shocked to realize that I recognized the names written on each one.

And then without being told, I knew exactly where I was. This lifeless room with its small files was a crude catalog system for my life. Here were written the actions of my every moment, big and small, in a detail my memory couldn't match.

A sense of wonder and curiosity, coupled with horror, stirred within me as I began randomly opening files and exploring their content. Some brought joy and sweet memories; others a sense of shame and regret so intense that I would look over my shoulder to see if anyone was watching. A file named 'Friends' was next to one marked 'Friends I Have Betrayed'.

The titles ranged from the mundane to the outright weird.

**HIS TREASURED POSSESSION**

'Books I Have Read', 'Lies I Have Told', 'Comfort I Have Given', 'Jokes I Have Laughed At'. Some were almost hilarious in their exactness: 'Things I've Yelled at My Brothers.' Others I couldn't laugh at: 'Things I Have Done in My Anger'. 'Things I Have Muttered Under My Breath at My Parents'. I never ceased to be surprised by the contents. Often there were many more cards than I expected. Sometimes fewer than I hoped.

I was overwhelmed by the sheer volume of the life I had lived. Could it be possible that I had the time in my 20 years to write each of these thousands or even millions of cards? But each card confirmed this truth. Each was written in my own handwriting. Each signed with my signature.

When I pulled out the file marked 'Songs I Have Listened To', I realized the files grew to contain their contents. The cards were packed tightly, and yet after two or three yards, I hadn't found the end of the file. I shut it, shamed, not so much by the quality of music, but more by the vast amount of time I knew that file represented.

When I came to a file marked 'Lust', I felt a chill run through my body. I pulled the file out only an inch, not willing to test its size, and drew out a card. I shuddered at its detailed content. I felt sick to think that such a moment had been recorded.

An almost animal rage broke on me. One thought dominated my mind: 'No one must ever see these cards! No one must ever see this room! I have to destroy them!' In an insane frenzy I yanked the file out. Its size didn't matter now. I had to empty it and burn the cards. But as I took it at one end and began pounding it on the floor, I could not dislodge a single card. I became desperate and pulled out a card, only to find it as strong as steel when I tried to tear it.

Defeated and utterly helpless, I returned the file to its slot. Leaning my forehead against the wall, I let out a long, self-pitying sigh. And then I saw it. The title bore 'People I Have Shared the Gospel With'. The handle was brighter than those around it, newer, almost unused. I pulled on its handle and a small box not more than three inches long fell into my hands. I could count the cards it contained on one hand.

And then the tears came. I began to weep. Sobs so deep that they hurt started in my stomach and shook through me. I fell on my knees and cried. I cried out of shame, from the overwhelming shame of it all. The rows of file shelves swirled in my tear-filled eyes. No one must ever, ever know of this room. I must lock it up and hide the key.

But then as I pushed away the tears, I saw Him. No, please not Him. Not here. Oh, anyone but Jesus.

I watched helplessly as He began to open the files and read the cards. I couldn't bear to watch His response. And in the moments I could bring myself to look at His face, I saw a sorrow deeper than my own. He seemed to intuitively go to the worst boxes. Why did He have to read every one?

Finally He turned and looked at me from across the room. He looked at me with pity in His eyes. But this was a pity that didn't anger me. I dropped my head, covered my face with my hands and began to cry again. He walked over and put His arm around me. He could have said so many things. But He didn't say a word. He just cried with me.

Then He got up and walked back to the wall of files.

Starting at one end of the room, He took out a file and, one by one, began to sign His name over mine on each card.

'No!' I shouted rushing to Him. All I could find to say was 'No, no,' as I pulled the card from Him. His name shouldn't be on these cards. But there it was, written in red so rich, so dark, so alive. The name of Jesus covered mine. It was written with His blood.

He gently took the card back. He smiled a sad smile and began to sign the cards. I don't think I'll ever understand how He did it so quickly, but the next instant it seemed I heard Him close the last file and walk back to my side. He placed His hand on my shoulder and said, 'It is finished.'

I stood up, and He led me out of the room. There was no lock on its door. There were still cards to be written.[1]

**Note**

1  By Joshua Harris. Quoted from TheReb, https://www.therebelution.com/blog/2006/10/the-room-by-joshua-harris/. Originally published in *New Attitude Magazine* © Copyright New Attitude 1995. As with any illustration of the cross, this one falls short.

# Appendix 10.
# A mix and match recipe

Here is an easy meal plan that you could use in offering hospitality. Don't be afraid to mix and match or to throw in a bit of this or that! In all my recipes, I just use whatever I have to hand.

## MEAT

- Lamb with tinned apricots
- Chicken with peppers
- Pork with onion and orange

Choose one of the above and place in a casserole or oven dish. Season with salt and pepper, and drizzle with olive oil.

## VEGETABLES

Then, in another oven dish or casserole, place sliced potatoes. Mix two or three eggs with about half a cup of milk and salt and pepper (increase the amount if you are catering for more than four people). Pour this mixture over the sliced potatoes.

In another casserole, place a mixture of other sliced vegetables (peppers, mushrooms, onions, tomatoes, courgette, etc.). Season with salt and pepper and drizzle with olive oil.

Place all three dishes (meat and vegetables) in the oven at gas mark 4–5 or 180–190 degrees C. Cook for 45 minutes, allowing each dish time on the top shelf to brown.

## PUDDING

- Get any fruit of your choice, fresh or tinned.

- Mix some muesli with 75–110 g (3–4 oz) of margarine.
- Sprinkle the muesli mixture over the fruit and cook for about 20 minutes at gas mark 5–6 (190–200 degrees C).

If there is room, you can place this dish in the oven to cook at the same time as the meat and vegetables. Just remember to get it out after about 20 minutes!

# Appendix 11. Discussion questions on hospitality

These questions, with suggested answers, are designed for personal or group use.

### 1. SHOULD EVERYONE BE INVOLVED IN HOSPITALITY?

(a) Yes.

(b) But there may be exceptions:

- The elderly: although I have known many eighty- and ninety-year-olds who have offered hospitality, such as a cup of coffee and a biscuit.

- Those with unbelieving spouses: although there are ways and means to encourage fellowship if you cannot invite Christians into your home. For example, you could make cakes and visit those who are house-bound or in nursing homes, or if your husband is at work have Christians round for a coffee (and a time of prayer).

- Those in real financial hardship: such people may be on the receiving end of hospitality until their circumstances change.

- Those who are unwell. Some may be physically or mentally incapable of preparing meals for others. I have known a number who are so stressed preparing a meal that they make themselves ill (I don't just mean those who get a bit worked up: in those cases, practice makes perfect, or near enough!).

## 2. WHAT ARE GOOD REASONS FOR OFFERING HOSPITALITY?

(a) It helps us get to know people better (relationships).

(b) It demonstrates love for people (loving).

(c) It can be a tool for evangelism (seeking).

(d) It can help those in the church who do not know many people (linking).

(e) It can help our children to strengthen ties with older people.

(f) It can be a great help to preachers, visitors or missionaries. Scriptural warrant for this is seen in Simon the tanner with Peter (Acts 9:43); Philemon (Philemon 22); Gaius (1) (Romans 16:23); Gaius (2) (3 John 5–8).

(g) It can help any who have special needs which might make them feel isolated, such as refugees, and those who are deaf or blind.

## 3. WHO SHOULD WE BE INVITING TO SHARE HOSPITALITY?

(a) Lonely, isolated people; for example, widows, singles (both men and women), single-parent families, divorcees, and Christians living with non-Christian families. They could be teenagers, students or older folk.

(b) People we do not naturally get along with.

(c) Groups of people who do not know one another very well in the church.

(d) People who are new to the church or passing through.

(e) Preachers or missionaries—maybe not just for a meal, but also to stay for a day or longer (not everyone will be able to offer this).

(f) Non-Christians: neighbours, friends or family (some or all who may be Christians), etc. Note that Jesus often taught round a table, e.g. woman anointing his feet, Zacchaeus; and with non-believers and believers.

## 4. WHAT ARE THE THINGS THAT MAY CAUSE PEOPLE TO FEEL THEY CANNOT OFFER HOSPITALITY?

(a) Time pressure: too many things to do.

(b) Finances. There may be genuine needs on the part of some. Those who may not be able to afford to give a meal could still give 'a cup of cold water'.

(c) Inadequate living conditions—although it is possible to share a house with someone else in order to host.

(d) Selfishness.

(e) Fear of failure ('. . . it's been modelled only at such a high standard that others feel they couldn't possibly do it like that').[1]

(f) Inexperience.

(g) Lack of discipline and organization, or failure to plan ahead.

(h) Pride.

(i) Others.

(j) Large, boisterous families.

## 5. ARE THERE PEOPLE TO WHOM WE SHOULD REFUSE TO OFFER HOSPITALITY?

(a) Those who have sinned and are unrepentant (1 Corinthians. 5:11; Matthew 18:15).

(b) We should not give lodging or money to false teachers to propagate their heresies (2 John 10–11). Some would say we should not even open our doors to them. But surely we should not ignore people who may come to our doors—what an opportunity that is! My husband and I have invited Mormons for a meal and Jehovah's Witnesses for coffee. In both cases, our desire was to evangelize. Where are they going to learn the truth if Christians shun them? Obviously, we would not give them board and lodging to enable them to propagate their error. This, I believe, is the gist of this command.

### 6. IN WHAT WAYS CAN WE BE THOUGHTFUL IN PRACTISING HOSPITALITY?

*When considering our families:*

(a) If someone in the family is ill.

(b) If children in the family have exams.

(c) If you have children, they may like to have their family to themselves sometimes, so hospitality could just be every other week or even once a month, or to suit your family circumstances.

(d) If your husband is a minister, he may have had a very busy week, so plan a Sunday when he is not preaching, or invite people on days other than Sundays.

*When considering others in the church:*

(a) If there is a single woman on her own, do not invite a single man on his own. By all means, invite him with a group.

(b) Think of those who have been on their own all week: Saturdays and Sundays can be difficult days for them, especially widows, widowers, single-parent families and divorcees.

(c) Consider the needs of different nationalities if it's within your ability, e.g. Bolognese for Italians, curries for Indians.

Make sure you say, 'It couldn't possibly be as good as yours, but I've tried'—that may mean a lot to them.

(d) People with special diets (e.g. vegetarian, gluten-free).

(e) Cook extra: a meal could be given to someone who is ill or just out of hospital.

(f) Invite several single people or youngsters—hospitality sometimes provides a meeting point for a number of students, singles or young people.

## 7. WHAT BENEFITS DO WE RECEIVE IF WE REGULARLY PRACTISE HOSPITALITY?

(a) We may receive unexpected blessings through our visitors. The Bible says that we may entertain 'angels without knowing it' (Hebrews 13:2).

(b) We receive blessing from God. It is Him we are inviting—e.g. 'if anyone gives even a cup of cold water . . . that person will certainly not lose their reward' (Matthew 10:42).

(c) For me, I feel richly rewarded to know that those who have been in our home have had a happy and blessed time. It is all worthwhile when there is mutual blessing.

## 8. WHAT DO WE LEARN FROM THIS VERSE: 'WHEN YOU GIVE A LUNCHEON OR DINNER, DO NOT INVITE YOUR FRIENDS, YOUR BROTHERS OR SISTERS, YOUR RELATIVES, OR YOUR RICH NEIGHBOURS; IF YOU DO, THEY MAY INVITE YOU BACK AND SO YOU WILL BE REPAID' (LUKE 14:12)?

This does not mean that we should not invite friends and family; it shows us that we are not to think only of them. There are other groups of people to invite, as we have discovered. We do not give in order to receive.

## 9. WHAT IS THE MOST IMPORTANT THING YOU HAVE LEARNED FROM THIS STUDY?

There are very few exemptions from giving hospitality.

**Note**

**1** Jones, *Cup of Cold Water*, p. 12.

# Appendix 12. Bible verses on hospitality

Matthew 25:35–36: 'For I was hungry and you gave me something to eat, I was thirsty and you gave me something to drink, I was a stranger and you invited me in, I needed clothes and you clothed me, I was ill and you looked after me, I was in prison and you came to visit me.'

Acts 16:15b: '. . . she invited us to her home. "If you consider me a believer in the Lord," she said, "come and stay at my house." And she persuaded us.'

Acts 21:8: 'We . . . stayed at the house of Philip the evangelist.'

Romans 12:13: 'Share with the Lord's people who are in need. Practise hospitality.'

Romans 16:23: 'Gaius, whose hospitality I and the whole church here enjoy, . . .'

1 Timothy 3:2: 'Now the overseer is to be . . . hospitable.'

1 Timothy 5:9–10: 'No widow may be put on the list of widows unless she is . . . well known for . . . showing hospitality.'

Hebrews 13:1–2: 'Keep on loving one another as brothers and sisters. Do not forget to show hospitality to strangers, for by so doing some people have shown hospitality to angels without knowing it.'

1 Peter 4:9: 'Offer hospitality to one another without grumbling.'

3 John 8: 'We ought therefore to show hospitality to such people [preachers] so that we may work together for the truth.'

# Appendix 13.
# Extract from Alexander Strauch, *The Hospitality Commands*

Here are two more examples of utter thoughtlessness with respect to hospitality.

While on vacation, my wife and I had the opportunity to visit a couple who had previously attended our church . . . but had since moved away. We were concerned about their spiritual welfare. We were delighted to learn that they were living for the Lord and were actively involved in a small local church. They had one complaint, however. During the past year that they had attended the church, not one person—not even one of the spiritual leaders—had invited them over for a meal or a time of fellowship. So, our friends still did not feel a part of the fellowship and were quite disheartened . . .

At times I have traveled as long as two or three hours on a Sunday morning in order to preach at a church. In some instances, when I finished speaking I was handed a check, invited to return, given many friendly handshakes, and bid a warm goodbye. But no one thought to invite me home for a meal, to provide rest before my long drive home, or to seek further fellowship with me after the Sunday morning service.[1]

### Note

1 Strauch, *Hospitality Commands*, p. 5.

# Appendix 14. Hallmarks of the Christian and the non-Christian

The first Epistle of John is very instructive with regard to 'tests' we can apply to our lives to determine whether or not we are Christians.

### 1:7 THE CHRISTIAN

'If we walk in the light, as he is in the light, we have fellowship with one another.'

### 1:6 THE NON-CHRISTIAN

'If we claim to have fellowship with him and yet walk in the darkness, we lie and do not live out the truth.'

### 1:9 THE CHRISTIAN

'If we confess our sins, he is faithful and just and will forgive us our sins.'

### 1:10 THE NON-CHRISTIAN

'If we claim we have not sinned, we make him out to be a liar and his word is not in us.'

### 2:3 THE CHRISTIAN

'We know that we have come to know him if we keep his commands.'

### 2:4 THE NON-CHRISTIAN

'Whoever says, "I know Him," but does not do what he commands is a liar, and the truth is not in that person.'

### 2:5B–6 THE CHRISTIAN

'This is how we know we are in him: whoever claims to live in him must live as Jesus did.'

### THE NON-CHRISTIAN

(Inference: They do not live as Jesus did.)

### 2:10 THE CHRISTIAN

'Anyone who loves their brother and sister lives in the light' (also 4:21).

### 2:9 THE NON-CHRISTIAN

'Anyone who claims to be in the light but hates a brother or sister is still in the darkness' (also 4:20).

### 2:15A THE CHRISTIAN

'Do not love the world or anything in the world.'

### 2:15B–16 THE NON-CHRISTIAN

'If anyone loves the world, love for the Father is not in them . . . [such love] comes not from the Father but from the world.'

### 2:17B THE CHRISTIAN

'Whoever does the will of God lives for ever.'

### THE NON-CHRISTIAN

'Anyone who hates a brother or sister is a murderer, and

you know that no murderer has eternal life residing in him'
(also 3:15).

### 2:19B THE CHRISTIAN

'If they had belonged to us, they would have remained with us.'

### 2:19A, 19B THE NON-CHRISTIAN

'They went out from us, but they did not really belong to
us . . . Their going showed that none of them belonged to us.'

### 2:23 THE CHRISTIAN

'Whoever acknowledges the Son has the Father also.'

### THE NON-CHRISTIAN

'No one who denies the Son has the Father.'

### 2:27B, 28A THE CHRISTIAN

'Remain in him . . . continue in him.'

### THE NON-CHRISTIAN

(Inference: They do not remain or continue in Him.)

### 2:29 THE CHRISTIAN

'Everyone who does what is right has been born of him.'

### NON-CHRISTIAN

(Inference: Everyone who does not do what is right is not
born of Him.)

### 3:6 THE CHRISTIAN

'No one who lives in him keeps on sinning.'

## HIS TREASURED POSSESSION

**THE NON-CHRISTIAN**

'No one who continues to sin has either seen him or known him.'

**3:7B–8 THE CHRISTIAN**

'The one who does what is right is righteous, just as he is righteous.'

**NON-CHRISTIAN**

'The one who does what is sinful is of the devil.'

**3:9 THE CHRISTIAN**

'No one who is born of God will continue to sin, because God's seed remains in them . . . they have been born of God' (also 5:18).

**3:10 NON-CHRISTIAN**

'Anyone who does not do what is right is not God's child, nor is anyone who does not love their brother and sister.'

**3:14 THE CHRISTIAN**

'We know that we have passed from death to life, because we love each other.'

**THE NON-CHRISTIAN**

'Anyone who does not love remains in death.'

**3:19, 22B THE CHRISTIAN**

'This is how we know that we belong to the truth . . . because we keep his commands and do what pleases him' (also 5:2–3).

[His commands = 'to believe in the name of his Son, Jesus Christ, and to love one another as he commanded us', 3:23]

### THE NON-CHRISTIAN

(Inference: They do not keep God's commands and do not love Christians.)

### 3:24 THE CHRISTIAN

'The one who keeps God's commands lives in him, and he in them . . . we know it by the Spirit he gave us' (also 4:13, 16).

### THE NON-CHRISTIAN

(Inference: They do not keep God's commands and do not know the Spirit of God.)

### 4:2–3A THE CHRISTIAN

'This is how you can recognise the Spirit of God: every spirit that acknowledges that Jesus Christ has come in the flesh is from God' (also 4:15–16).

### THE NON-CHRISTIAN

'But every spirit that does not acknowledge Jesus is not from God.'

### 4:6 THE CHRISTIAN

'We are from God, and whoever knows God listens to us . . . This is how we recognise the Spirit of truth and the spirit of falsehood.'

### THE NON-CHRISTIAN

'But whoever is not from God does not listen to us.'

## HIS TREASURED POSSESSION

### 4:7 THE CHRISTIAN

'Let us love one another, for love comes from God. Everyone who loves has been born of God and knows God.'

### 4:8 THE NON-CHRISTIAN

'Whoever does not love does not know God, because God is love.'

### 5:4 THE CHRISTIAN

'Everyone born of God overcomes the world.'

### THE NON-CHRISTIAN

(Inference: Everyone not born of God does not overcome the world.)

### 5:10–11 THE CHRISTIAN

'Whoever believes . . . accepts this testimony . . . And this is the testimony: God has given us eternal life, and this life is in his Son.'

### THE NON-CHRISTIAN

'Whoever does not believe God has made him out to be a liar, because they have not believed the testimony God has given about his Son.'

### 5:12 THE CHRISTIAN

'Whoever has the Son has life.'

### THE NON-CHRISTIAN

'Whoever does not have the Son of God does not have life.'

# Select bibliography

Alcorn, Randy, *The Treasure Principle: Unlocking the Secret of Joyful Giving* (Portland, OR: Multnomah, 2001).

Beeke, Joel R., and Derek W. H. Thomas, *The Holy Spirit and Reformed Spirituality* (Grand Rapids, MI: Reformation Heritage Books, 2013).

St Bernard, 'Sermon 6. God's Infinite Power, Mercy and Judgment', in *Commentary on the Song of Solomon*, Archive.org, https://archive.org/stream/StBernardsCommentaryOnTheSongOfSongs/StBernardOnTheSongOfSongsall_djvu.txt.

Bonar, Andrew A., *Reminiscences of Andrew A. Bonar D.D.* (London: Hodder and Stoughton, 1895). Online at https://archive.org/stream/reminiscencesofaoobonauoft/reminiscencesofaoobonauoft_djvu.txt.

———, *Memoirs and Remains of R. M. M'Cheyne* (Edinburgh: Banner of Truth Trust, 1973).

Bridges, Jerry, *The Practice of Godliness* (Colorado Springs, CO: NavPress, 2008).

Brooks, Thomas, *Precious Remedies Against Satan's Devices* (Edinburgh: Banner of Truth Trust, 1968).

Bunyan, John, *The Pilgrim's Progress in Today's English* (Eastbourne: Kingsway, 1972).

Butterfield, Rosaria Champagne, *The Secret Thoughts of an Unlikely Convert* (Pittsburgh: Crown & Covenant, 2012).

Calvin, John, *Calvin's Calvinism; Part 1: A Treatise on the Eternal*

*Predestination of God*, trans. Henry. P. Cole (London: Kessinger Publishing, 2010).

Calvin, John, *Institutes of the Christian Religion*, Volume 1 (Grand Rapids, MI: Eerdmans, 1979).

Cecil, Richard, *Remains of the Rev. Richard Cecil* (Andover: Mark Newman, 1824).

Cowman, Chas. E. *Streams in the Desert* ([USA]: Cowman Publications, 1959).

Davies, Andrew, 'Time and Eternity: The Puritan Outlook', in *Westminster Conference 1999: God Is Faithful*, Puritan Papers (Stoke-on-Trent: Westminster Conference, 2000).

De Young, Kevin, *A Hole in Our Holiness: Filling the Gap between Gospel Passion and the Pursuit of Godliness* (Wheaton, IL: Crossway, 2012).

Drummond, Henry, *The New Evangelism and Other Essays* (New York: Dodd, Mead and Company, 1899).

Eareckson Tada, Joni, *Heaven: Your Real Home* (Grand Rapids, MI: Zondervan, 2010).

Edwards, Jonathan, *Christian Love and Its Fruits* (Lafayette, IN: Sovereign Grace, 2001).

Elliot, Elisabeth, *Wesleyan Advocate*, 20 June 1977.

Gilbert, Josiah Hotchkiss, *Dictionary of Burning Words of Brilliant Writers* (New York: W. B. Ketcham, 1895).

Gumbel, Nicky, *Questions of Life* (Eastbourne: Kingsway, 1995).

Havner, Vance, *The Chosen Path: 365 Inspirational Messages* *(Bloomington, IN: Elm Hill Books, 2005)*.

Jeffery, Peter, *I Will Never Become a Christian* (Bridgend: Evangelical Press of Wales, 1994).

Jenkins, Christopher, 'Thomas Watson and How to Live a Godly Life', in *The Power of God in the Life of Man*, Westminster Conference papers (Stoke-on-Trent: Tentmaker Publications, 2005).

Jones, Julia, *A Cup of Cold Water* (Leominster: Day One, 2006).

King, Coretta Scott, *The Words of Martin Luther King, Jr*, 2nd edn (New York: Harper Collins, 2011).

Lane, Timothy S., and Paul David Tripp, *Change Is Possible*, 2nd edn (Greensboro, NC: New Growth Press, 2008).

MacMillan, J. Douglas, *The Lord Our Shepherd* (Bridgend: Evangelical Press of Wales, 1983).

Manley Pippert, Rebecca, *Out of the Saltshaker: Evangelism as a Way of Life* (Leicester: Inter-Varsity Press, 1979).

Moody, D. L., *Prevailing Prayer* (Chicago: Moody, 2015).

Morgan, Hugh, *Holy God, Holy People* (Bridgend: Bryntirion, 2007).

Müller, George, *Autobiography of George Müller, or A Million and a Half in Answer to Prayer*, 3rd edn (London: J. Nisbet *and Co., 1914)*.

Murray, John, *Collected Writings of John Murray*, Volume 2: *Systematic Theology* (Edinburgh: Banner of Truth Trust, 1977).

————, *Principles of Conduct* (Grand Rapids, MI: Eerdmans, 1977)

Owen, John, *The Person of Christ* (Lafayette, IN: Sovereign Grace, 2001).

Packer, J. I., *Finishing Our Course with Joy: Ageing with Hope* (Nottingham: Inter-Varsity Press, 2014).

———, *Keep in Step with the Spirit* (Leicester: Inter-Varsity Press, 1984).

———, *Knowing God* (London: Hodder and Stoughton, 1975).

Pierson, Arthur T., *George Müller of Bristol* (Bromley: Send the Light Trust, 1973).

Pink, Arthur W., *The Sovereignty of God* (Pensacola, FL: Chapel Library, 2014).

Piper, John, *Desiring God: Meditations of a Christian Hedonist*, 10th expanded edn (Colorado Springs, CO: Multnomah, 1996).

Piper, John, *Desiring God: Meditations of a Christian Hedonist*, rev. edn (Colorado Springs, CO: Multnomah, 2011).

Prime, Samuel, *The Power of Prayer: The New York Revival of 1858* (Edinburgh: Banner of Truth Trust, 1991).

Prior, K. F., *Great Doctrines of the Bible: The Way of Holiness* (London: Inter-Varsity Fellowship, 1967).

Richmond, Legh, *The Dairyman's Daughter and Other Annals of the Poor* ([England]: Gospel Standard Baptist Trust, 1976).

Roberts, Maurice, *Great God of Wonders* (Edinburgh: Banner of Truth Trust, 2003).

———, *The Thought of God* (Edinburgh: Banner of Truth Trust, 1995).

Ryle, J. C., *Expository Thoughts on St Matthew* (Ipswich: William Hunt and Company, 1878).

———, *Holiness* (Welwyn: Evangelical Press, 1979).

Schaeffer, Edith, *What Is a Family?* (London: Hodder and Stoughton, 1978).

Schaeffer, Francis, *Escape from Reason: A Penetrating Analysis of Trends in Modern Thought* (Downers Grove, IL: InterVarsity Press, 1968).

Sproul, R. C., *The Holiness of God (Carol Stream, IL: Tyndale House, 1985)*.

Spurgeon, Charles Haddon, *The Early Years: Volume 1* (Edinburgh: Banner of Truth Trust, 1973).

———, *The Soul Winner* (London: Passmore & Alabaster, 1905).

———, *The Soul Winner* (Lafayette, IN: Sovereign Grace, 2001).

Stott, John, *Christian Basics: A Handbook of Christian Faith* (London: Hodder & Stoughton, 1991).

Strauch, Alexander, *The Hospitality Commands* (Littleton, CO: Lewis and Roth 2010).

Thomas, John, *Contender for the Faith* (Bridgend: Evangelical Movement of Wales, 1975).

Watson, Thomas, *A Body of Divinity* (Edinburgh: Banner of Truth Trust, 1974).

———, *The Christian Soldier: Or Heaven Taken by Storm, Shewing the Holy Violence a Christian Is to Put Forth in the Pursuit after Glory* (New York: Robert Moore, 1810).

————, *A Divine Cordial: An Exposition of Romans 8:28* (London: Sovereign Grace, 2018).

————, *The Godly Man's Picture* (repr.; Carlisle, PA: Banner of Truth Trust, 2013).

Whitney, Donald S., *Spiritual Disciplines for the Christian Life* ([UK]: Scripture Press, 1993).

Wright, N. T., *John for Everyone; Part 2: Chapters 11–21* (London: SPCK, 2002).